QUICK FROM SCRATCH
ITALIAN

White-Bean and Prosciutto Bruschetta, page 27

QUICK FROM SCRATCH
ITALIAN

Food & Wine
BOOKS

American Express Publishing Corporation
New York

Editor in Chief: Judith Hill

Art Director: Nina Scerbo	**Associate Editor:** Susan Lantzius Rich
Managing Editor: Terri Mauro	**Assistant Editor:** Laura Byrne Russell
Copy Editor: Barbara A. Mateer	**Editorial Assistant:** Evette Manners
Wine Editor: Steve Miller	**Photographer:** Melanie Acevedo
Food Stylist: Rori Spinelli	**Prop Stylist:** Robyn Glaser
Portrait Photographer: Chris Dinerman	**Production Manager:** Stuart Handelman

Senior Vice President/Chief Marketing Officer: Mark V. Stanich
Vice President, Books, Products, and Services: Bruce Rosner
Director, Branded Services and Retail Sales: Marshall A. Corey
Operations Manager: Phil Black
Business Manager: Doreen Camardi

Cover Design: Perri DeFino and Elizabeth Rendfleisch
Recipe Pictured on Front Cover: Orecchiette with Broccoli Rabe, Bacon, and Bread Crumbs, page 73

AMERICAN EXPRESS PUBLISHING CORPORATION
©1998, 2002 American Express Publishing Corporation

LIBRARY OF CONGRESS CATALOGING-IN-PUBLICATION DATA
Quick from scratch. Italian.
p. cm.
Includes index.
ISBN 0-916103-41-2 (hardcover)—ISBN 0-916103-79-X (softcover)
1. Cookery, Italian 2. Quick and easy cookery. I. Food & wine (New York, N.Y.)
TX723.Q53 1998
641.5945—dc21 97-41317
CIP

Published by American Express Publishing Corporation
1120 Avenue of the Americas, New York, New York 10036

Manufactured in the United States of America

CONTENTS

RECIPES PICTURED ABOVE: *(left to right)* pages 69, 89, 153

Sampling Minestrone with Arborio Rice, page 33, in FOOD & WINE Books' test kitchen.

Susan Lantzius Rich trained at La Varenne École de Cuisine in Paris, worked as a chef in Portugal for a year, and then headed to New York City. There she made her mark first as head decorator at the well-known Sant Ambroeus pastry shop and next as a pastry chef, working at such top restaurants as San Domenico and Maxim's. In 1993, she turned her talents to recipe development and editorial work for FOOD & WINE Books.

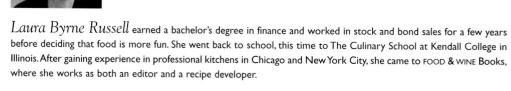

Judith Hill is the editor in chief of FOOD & WINE Books, a division of American Express Publishing. Previously she was editor in chief of COOK'S Magazine, director of publications for La Varenne École de Cuisine in Paris, from which she earned a Grand Diplôme, and an English instructor for the University of Maryland International Division in Germany. Her book credits include editing cookbooks for Fredy Girardet, Jane Grigson, Michel Guérard, and Anne Willan.

Laura Byrne Russell earned a bachelor's degree in finance and worked in stock and bond sales for a few years before deciding that food is more fun. She went back to school, this time to The Culinary School at Kendall College in Illinois. After gaining experience in professional kitchens in Chicago and New York City, she came to FOOD & WINE Books, where she works as both an editor and a recipe developer.

ITALIAN ALCHEMY

During the week, when time is short, I'm more likely to cook Italian than any other cuisine. When I'm entertaining and want to serve something that's absolutely dependable and sure to please, Italian dishes top my list. And when I take people out for lunch or dinner, especially when I don't know their taste, I feel safer choosing an Italian restaurant than any other kind—even American. Italian cooking has become America's cuisine of choice. Why? That's easy to answer: Italian food is reliably simple and fresh, both currently prized attributes. And, of course, it tastes great.

The Italians have a magical flair for transforming a short, seemingly uninspired list of ingredients into a bewitching dish. Little more than olive oil, salt, and pepper conjure up the most delectable food. **Risi e Bisi** (page 35), for example, shows how divine rice and peas can become with a wave of the Italian wand. **Veal Chops Milanese** (page 111) are made special with just a bit of sage in the bread-crumb coating and a squirt of lemon juice at the end. Coffee, cream, and sugar become the tantalizing **Espresso Granita with Whipped Cream** (page 169). It's nothing short of alchemy—common ingredients turned into gold.

When you're eating in Italy, it's tempting to trace the source of all this sorcery to the remarkable produce and other foodstuffs so abundant there. But the time-honored formulas of Italian cuisine work in our own country, too, and with plain-old supermarket ingredients. As editors Susan Rich, Laura Russell, and I tasted the recipes during the development stage of this book, we were delighted daily. Susan, who did most of the cooking for this volume of the series, could do no wrong. I attribute a good portion of the explanation for this success to her exceptional prowess in the kitchen, but we all three agreed that Italian wizardry was at work, too.

There are so many good ideas in Italian cooking that we had a grand time choosing and honing the most appropriate dishes from the traditional specialties of all the various regions of the country. Quick pasta dishes, straightforward grills, the simplest of sauces, labor-light fruit desserts—these are all hallmarks of Italian cuisine. When good cooking is so easy, how can we help but love it?

Judith Hill
Editor in Chief
FOOD & WINE Books

Before You Begin

In this opening section, we've gathered thoughts and tips that apply to all, or at least a substantial number, of the recipes in this book. These are the facts and opinions that we'd like you to know before you use the recipes and to keep in mind while you use them. In addition to test-kitchen tips, you'll find information about wines, cheeses, and the typical Italian meal.

PORTION SIZES

A traditional Italian dinner includes a number of courses, each offering a moderate portion, as opposed to one large main dish. The first course is usually soup, pasta, or rice followed by a fish, chicken, or meat second course, often accompanied by vegetables. Salad comes after the second course. Although antipasti and dessert appear at more lavish, special-occasion meals, for everyday dinners antipasti is often skipped and dessert is usually fresh or simply cooked fruit.

With busy workdays and conflicting schedules, Italians and Americans alike often do not have enough time to enjoy a leisurely multicourse meal. We've developed this book with that in mind, and so all of our recipes (excluding antipasti and desserts) are meant to serve as a main dish for four people—even the soups, pasta, and rice dishes.

If you'd like to use the recipes to host a more traditional Italian meal for your family or friends, start with an antipasto or several of them, choose a first course from the soup, pasta, or rice chapter, follow it with a chicken, meat, or fish recipe, and end the meal with one of our delicious, easy Italian desserts. In this case, the first-course recipes will serve six.

RECIPES PICTURED OPPOSITE: (top) pages 127, 19, 125; (center) pages 63, 129, 22; (bottom) pages 17, 35, 171

Faster, Better, Easier
TEST-KITCHEN TIPS

Quick no-cook antipasti

You can put together an impressive antipasti platter in minutes with a few choice deli items and pantry staples. Serve the antipasti as an appetizer or even as an informal meal.

■ Cured meats—thin slices of prosciutto, coppa, *soppressata*, hard salami, or other dried sausages

■ Cheeses—shaved Parmigiano-Reggiano or Asiago, wedges of goat cheese, balls of fresh mozzarella marinated in olive oil and herbs, slices of Taleggio or provolone

■ Other possibilities—green or black olives, canned tuna, sliced or grated raw vegetables dressed with olive oil, pickled vegetables (*giardiniera*), sliced melon or figs

Soup too thick?

Many Italian-style soups are so chock-full of rice or pasta that much of the liquid is absorbed before the soup hits the table. To thin the soup before serving, simply stir in some extra broth or water. Taste the soup and add more salt and pepper if necessary.

Pasta cooking tips

■ Cook pasta in lots of boiling, salted water. Count on using at least three quarts of water and one-and-a-half tablespoons of salt to cook three-quarters of a pound of pasta.

■ When the water boils, add the pasta all at once and stir. Don't break long strands of pasta in half to make them fit, just ease them in slowly. Stir the pasta frequently as it cooks.

■ Before draining the pasta, ladle out some of the cooking water to save in case the sauce is too thick. Pasta-cooking water thins a sauce and adds a bit of flavor at the same time.

■ Cooking times for pasta are merely guidelines. To check for doneness, bite into a piece of pasta. It should be slightly chewy. Look at the center of the bitten piece; there should be no opaque white core. Retest frequently.

■ Drain the pasta and immediately toss it with the sauce. Never rinse pasta unless you're serving it cold, as in a salad, or letting it stand a while undressed, as when constructing lasagne.

Reviving Parmesan cheese

If a wedge of Parmesan is drying out, wrap it in a damp paper towel and then in plastic wrap or aluminum foil. Refrigerate. A day later, remove the paper towel, rewrap tightly, and store in the refrigerator.

Making risotto

Perfectly cooked risotto is not at all difficult to make; you just need to keep a few important tips in mind.

- Use short- or medium-grain rice; arborio is the easiest to find.
- Stir the rice in hot fat until it's well coated before adding any liquid to the pan.
- Add hot liquid to the rice a little at a time; don't add more until the previous addition is absorbed.
- Keep the liquid at a simmer and stir the rice often.
- The amount of liquid you need to cook the rice may differ slightly from the amount called for in a recipe. Adjust the quantity if necessary to cook the rice and have some thickened liquid left as a sauce.

The fish and cheese taboo

Although there are exceptions to every rule (and we make a few of them), fish and cheese are rarely served together in Italy. In fact, fish is seldom combined with any dairy product. To top shrimp risotto with Parmesan, for example, would be considered a heresy.

Cooking vegetables, Italian style

Italy grows arguably the best produce in the world, and fresh, seasonal vegetables are a mainstay of the Italian diet. When cooking them, Italians do not hold crunchiness as a goal. They cook vegetables until they're tender (but not overcooked) so the flavor reaches its peak.

Dressing salads

While a perfectly emulsified vinaigrette is important in classic French cuisine, the Italian salad is slightly more relaxed. Simply put the lettuce in a serving bowl, toss with extra-virgin olive oil, salt, and pepper, and then toss again with the vinegar. Taste a piece of lettuce and adjust any seasonings.

Storing fresh basil

Basil leaves have a tendency to turn black quickly in the refrigerator. To make the herb last longer, store a bunch in a jar with enough water to cover the stem ends or roots and then put a plastic bag over the leaves. Or, wrap a wet paper towel around the bottom of the bunch and then cover the entire thing with plastic wrap and refrigerate.

Beloved bread

Italians rarely waste even a single crumb of bread. To recycle bread the Italian way, grill day-old slices for bruschetta; fry cubes in oil with garlic for croutons; run leftover bread in the food processor with the regular blade to make fresh bread crumbs; or toast the fresh bread crumbs in the oven and process them again to make fine dry bread crumbs.

ITALIAN WINES

	TYPE	WINE	DESCRIPTION	FOOD AFFINITY
White	Light, crisp, neutral	• Gavi • Orvieto • Pinot grigio • Soave • Verdicchio	Light body and delicate flavor with good acidity. Made to highlight food, not conflict. Flavors include floral, herbal, nutty, and subtle apple notes.	Light fish and chicken dishes. Salads. Can handle light tomato sauces.
	Medium, fruity	• Chardonnay • Pinot bianco • Sauvignon blanc • Vernaccia di San Gimignano	Richer and fuller with more obvious fruit flavor. Chardonnay is more spicy, while sauvignon blanc and vernaccia are more herbal or nutty.	Richer fish and chicken dishes. Veal. Salads. More highly spiced and herbed foods. Be careful with chardonnay: It is often oaky and can overpower many foods.
	Full, rich	• Fiano di Avellino • Gewürztraminer • Greco di Tufo • Tocai Friulano	Full-bodied wines that can overpower a subtle dish. Earthy, nutty, honey, and spicy flavors.	Rich full-flavored fish, chicken, veal, and pork dishes.
Rosé	Medium, fruity	• Lacryma Christi	Full-bodied with delicate strawberry and earthy flavors.	Garlicky and salty foods. Seafood with tomato sauce. Smoked meats; prosciutto.
Red	Light, fruity	• Bardolino • Chianti • Dolcetto d'Asti • Grignolino • Valpolicella	Simple, grapey, high-acid wines for everyday drinking.	Pasta with tomato sauce. Pizza. Chicken. Light-flavored red-meat dishes.
	Medium, rich	• Barbera • Carmignano • Chianti Riserva • Dolcetto d'Alba • Franciacorta • Montepulciano d'Abruzzo • Refosco • Rosso di Montalcino • Salice Salentino • Valtellina	More substantial wines with subtle fruitiness and some earthy and herbal flavors. Moderately tannic.	Rich tomato sauce. Pork, veal, and red meats. Braised poultry and meats. Stews.
	Full, rich, complex	• Barbaresco • Barolo • Brunello • Vino Nobile di Montepulciano	Italy's most revered wines. Powerful; structured for long-term development with complex, multidimensional flavors.	Should be showcased by serving with simply prepared red meat, such as steaks, chops, and roasts.

—STEVE MILLER

ITALIAN CHEESES

TEXTURE	CHEESE	MILK	DESCRIPTION
Soft curd	Ricotta	Sheep's, water buffalo's, or goat's (Italy); cow's (U.S.)	Produced from the whey left over from cheesemaking. Mild in flavor and relatively low in fat. The original Italian version has a drier texture than that produced in the United States.
Soft	Mascarpone	Cow's	Lusciously rich, much like French crème fraîche or English clotted cream. Delicate flavor lends itself graciously to either savory or sweet dishes.
Semisoft	Gorgonzola	Cow's	One of the great blue cheeses of the world. Blue-green veined, full flavored, and creamy in texture. There are two types: Sweet is softer and milder tasting; aged is a bit firmer and bolder flavored.
	Mozzarella	Water buffalo's or cow's (Italy); cow's (U.S.)	Fresh mozzarella has a mild, milky taste and is available salted, unsalted, and smoked. Fairly soft texture but not rubbery like that made by big manufacturers.
	Taleggio	Cow's	Square in shape. Full flavored and buttery when ripe. It doesn't quite run when cut into; it bulges.
Semifirm	Fontina	Cow's	Italian fontina is a marvelous melting cheese, with a distinctive nutty taste. Scandinavian fontina is okay, but not exceptional.
Firm	Asiago	Cow's	Mild in flavor. As it ages and hardens it develops more of a bite and is good for grating.
	Provolone	Cow's	Mild-mannered at first. Sharper flavored with age, becoming quite provocative after about a year.
Hard	Parmigiano-Reggiano	Cow's	Real Parmigiano-Reggiano is aged for at least fourteen months and has its name stamped on the rind. Avoid any imposters in a canister.
	Pecorino Romano	Sheep's (Italy); cow's (U.S.)	Great grating cheese, often substituted for Parmesan. Sharp, intense, relatively salty flavor. The Italian sheep's cheese is fuller and more distinctive.

CHAPTER ONE

Antipasti

ROASTED PEPPERS WITH CAPER DRESSING

A plate of red and yellow bell peppers tossed with a tangy dressing pleases both the eye and the palate. You can use peppers of only one color, if you prefer, or include an orange and a green bell pepper for a truly spectacular effect.

SERVES 4

2   red bell peppers

2   yellow bell peppers

½   teaspoon lemon juice

¾   teaspoon anchovy paste

1½   teaspoons wine vinegar

¾   teaspoon salt

¼   teaspoon fresh-ground black pepper

¼   cup olive oil

2   tablespoons drained capers

1.   Roast the peppers over a gas flame or grill or broil them, turning with tongs, until charred all over, about 10 minutes. When the peppers are cool enough to handle, pull off the skin. Remove the stems, seeds, and ribs. Cut the peppers lengthwise into ½-inch strips.

2.   In a large glass or stainless-steel bowl, using a fork, stir together the lemon juice, anchovy paste, vinegar, salt, and pepper. Stir in the oil. Add the peppers and capers and toss.

VARIATIONS

■ Use halved and pitted **olives** in addition to or instead of the capers.
■ Add a sprinkling of chopped fresh **basil**.
■ Toss in a chopped **tomato**.
■ Use three chopped **anchovy fillets** instead of the paste.
■ Add a small can of drained **tuna**.

SHORTCUT

To roast the peppers quickly and with little mess, stand them upright and cut the flesh from each of the four sides, leaving the stem, seeds, and core behind. Put the peppers on an aluminum-foil-lined baking sheet, cut-side down, and broil until charred. Peel off the blackened skin.

MUSHROOMS WITH LEMON DRESSING

Don't skip over this excellent antipasto because of the anchovy paste; only the cook will know it's there. There's no fishy taste at all, just exceptionally flavorful mushrooms and a bright, lemony tang.

SERVES 4

4 teaspoons lemon juice

½ teaspoon anchovy paste

½ teaspoon salt

½ teaspoon fresh-ground black pepper

5 tablespoons olive oil

1¼ pounds mushrooms, cut into ⅛-inch slices

3 tablespoons chopped fresh parsley

In a large glass or stainless-steel bowl, using a fork, stir together the lemon juice, anchovy paste, salt, and pepper. Stir in the oil. Add the mushrooms and parsley and toss.

CARROTS WITH PINE NUTS AND BASIL

Slender strips of sweet carrot take a brief dip in boiling water and then join rich toasted pine nuts and refreshing basil in an ideal combination. Grate the carrots in a food processor or by hand, whichever seems easier.

SERVES 4

¼ cup pine nuts

6 carrots (about 1 pound), peeled and grated

1¼ teaspoons lemon juice

¼ teaspoon salt

1½ tablespoons olive oil

2 tablespoons thin-sliced basil leaves

1. In a small frying pan, toast the pine nuts over moderately low heat, stirring frequently, until golden brown, about 5 minutes. Or toast the pine nuts in a 350° oven for 5 to 10 minutes. Let cool.

2. In a large pot of boiling water, cook the carrots for just 30 seconds. Drain the carrots, rinse with cold water, and drain thoroughly. Toss the carrots with the lemon juice, salt, oil, pine nuts, and basil.

FENNEL AND RED-ONION SALAD WITH PARMESAN

Crisp raw fennel, pungent onion, and a sprightly lemon and orange dressing make for a delectable salad. A food processor with a slicing attachment cuts the fennel in no time.

SERVES 4

- 2 tablespoons lemon juice
- ¾ teaspoon grated orange zest
- 1½ tablespoons fresh orange juice
- ¾ teaspoon salt
- ¼ teaspoon fresh-ground black pepper
- 6 tablespoons olive oil
- 1¾ pounds fennel bulbs (about 2 large), cored and shaved as thin as possible
- 1 small red onion, chopped fine
- ½ cup grated Parmesan, or a chunk of Parmesan for making curls

1. In a large glass or stainless-steel bowl, whisk together the lemon juice, orange zest, orange juice, salt, and ⅛ teaspoon of the pepper. Add the oil slowly, whisking. Add the fennel and onion and toss. Let stand at least 5 minutes but no more than 1 hour.

2. To serve, top the salad with the grated Parmesan, or with a few curls of Parmesan shaved from the chunk of cheese using a vegetable peeler. Sprinkle with the remaining ⅛ teaspoon pepper.

VARIATION

In addition to the orange zest and juice, add the **segments** from one **orange** to the salad. Using a stainless-steel knife, peel the orange down to the flesh, removing all of the white pith. Cut the sections away from the membranes. Squeeze the juice from the membranes to use in the dressing.

SLICING FENNEL BY HAND

If you are slicing fennel by hand, the easiest way is to cut off the stalks, cut the bulb in half from the top through the root end, lay each half flat-side down, and slice crosswise.

GRILLED ZUCCHINI WITH FRESH MOZZARELLA

The delicate taste of fresh mozzarella offers a delicious counterpoint to the garlic-and-vinegar-macerated zucchini. However, if you prefer a stronger cheese flavor, try goat cheese instead.

SERVES 4

- 3 zucchini (about 1 pound), cut lengthwise into 1/4-inch slices
- 2 tablespoons olive oil
   Salt
   Fresh-ground black pepper
- 1/4 teaspoon wine vinegar
- 1 clove garlic, minced
- 1 tablespoon chopped flat-leaf parsley
- 1/2 pound salted fresh mozzarella, cut into thick slices

1. Light the grill or heat the broiler. In a large glass or stainless-steel bowl, toss the zucchini with 1 tablespoon of the oil, 1/4 teaspoon salt, and 1/8 teaspoon pepper. Grill or broil the zucchini, turning once, until tender and golden, about 5 minutes per side. Put the zucchini back in the bowl.

2. Toss the zucchini with 1/2 tablespoon of the oil, 1/8 teaspoon salt, the vinegar, garlic, and parsley. Let cool.

3. Put the mozzarella slices on a serving plate, fanning them out to form a circle. Drizzle them with the remaining 1/2 tablespoon oil and sprinkle them with a pinch of pepper. Fold the zucchini slices in half and tuck them between the pieces of cheese.

FRESH MOZZARELLA

Soft mozzarella is shaped into balls and stored in water to keep it moist. It is available both salted and unsalted, but the latter is very bland indeed. We prefer the salted variety; salting brings out the mild, milky flavor of the cheese.

Bruschetta Duet

We like the variety here—the same toast spread with two different toppings. The green-olive tapenade, which uses pre-pitted olives, can be made in minutes with a blender or food processor. The sautéed mushroom topping is equally savory hot or at room temperature.

SERVES 4

8 tablespoons olive oil

2 teaspoons butter

¾ pound mushrooms, chopped fine

3 cloves garlic, 2 minced, 1 smashed

¼ teaspoon salt

Fresh-ground black pepper

¼ teaspoon dried sage

1 tablespoon chopped flat-leaf parsley, plus ⅓ cup lightly packed leaves

½ cup pitted green olives

½ teaspoon anchovy paste

1½ teaspoons lemon juice

Bruschetta, opposite

1. In a large frying pan, heat 2 tablespoons of the oil with the butter over moderately high heat. Add the mushrooms, the minced garlic, the salt, ⅛ teaspoon pepper, and the sage. Cook, stirring occasionally, until the mushrooms are golden, 5 to 10 minutes. Stir in the chopped parsley. Remove from the heat.

2. In a blender or food processor, put the olives, parsley leaves, smashed garlic, anchovy paste, the remaining 6 tablespoons olive oil, the lemon juice, and ¼ teaspoon pepper. Blend or process to a coarse puree.

3. Spread the mushroom mixture on eight of the bruschetta, and the tapenade on the rest.

Bruschetta

MAKES 16 BRUSCHETTA

4 ½-inch-thick slices country bread

2 tablespoons olive oil

⅛ teaspoon salt

1. Heat the broiler. Put the bread on a baking sheet and brush both sides with the oil. Sprinkle with the salt.

2. Broil, turning once, until the bread is brown on the outside but still slightly soft in the center, about 3 minutes. Alternatively (and more traditionally), grill the bread. Cut each slice of bread into quarters.

White-Bean and Prosciutto Bruschetta

Strips of prosciutto top each toast and are topped in turn with a mound of creamy white beans and a sprinkling of crisp red onion. If you like, serve these with the Bruschetta Duet on page 25 to make a tantalizing trio.

SERVES 4

2 cups drained and rinsed canned cannellini beans (one 19-ounce can)

1¼ teaspoons wine vinegar

1 tablespoon olive oil

¾ teaspoon chopped fresh thyme, or ¼ teaspoon dried thyme

¼ teaspoon salt

⅛ teaspoon fresh-ground black pepper

2½ tablespoons chopped fresh parsley

2 ounces thin-sliced prosciutto, fat removed, cut into thin strips

Bruschetta, page 25

2 tablespoons minced red onion

1. Put the beans in a medium glass or stainless-steel bowl. Using a fork, mash the beans to a coarse puree. Stir in the vinegar, oil, thyme, salt, pepper, and 2 tablespoons of the parsley.

2. Put some of the prosciutto on each of the bruschetta and top with the bean mixture. Sprinkle the remaining ½ tablespoon parsley and the red onion over the beans.

Variations

Bruschetta can be topped with endless combinations of ingredients. Some of our favorites to try:
- Chopped **tomato** and **basil**
- Diced **roasted bell peppers** with crumbled **goat cheese**
- Drained canned **tuna** and **capers**
- Strips of **Parmigiano-Reggiano**
- A split **garlic** clove rubbed over the toast, followed by a generous drizzle of **olive oil**

SHRIMP MARINATED IN LEMON AND OLIVE OIL

You'll want to gobble up these succulent morsels immediately, but patience will be rewarded; the shrimp taste better the longer they sit in the marinade. Leave them for a couple of hours, if you have the time.

SERVES 4

1   pound large shrimp, in their shells

3½   teaspoons lemon juice

2   tablespoons olive oil

1   tomato, seeded and cut into ¼-inch dice

¼   teaspoon salt

⅛   teaspoon fresh-ground black pepper

2   tablespoons chopped fresh parsley

1. Bring a large pot of salted water to a boil. Add the shrimp, cover, and bring back to a boil. Continue boiling, partially covered, until the shrimp are just done, 1 to 2 minutes. Drain. Let the shrimp cool and then peel them.

2. In a large glass or stainless-steel bowl, combine the lemon juice with the olive oil, tomato, salt, pepper, and parsley. Add the shrimp and toss.

VARIATIONS

■ Substitute a pound of **sea scallops** for the shrimp. Heat one tablespoon of oil in a large nonstick frying pan over moderately high heat until very hot. Season the scallops with one-eighth teaspoon salt. Put the scallops in the pan and sear until brown on the bottom, one to two minutes. Turn and brown on the other side until just done, one to two minutes longer. Remove the scallops and cut them into quarters. Toss with the marinade.

■ Spice up the dish by adding one-quarter teaspoon dried **red-pepper flakes** to the marinade.

■ Use chopped fresh **basil** instead of the parsley.

■ For an extra flavor dimension, add a clove of minced **garlic** to the marinade.

CHAPTER TWO

Main-Course Soups

MINESTRONE WITH ARBORIO RICE

There are as many versions of minestrone as there are cooks in Italy, but the soup always contains a wide variety of vegetables and usually includes beans and either pasta or rice. If you happen to have the rind from a chunk of Parmigiano-Reggiano, throw that into the soup pot as well. The arborio rice here soaks up and also thickens the liquid; if the soup gets too thick, don't hesitate to add water or more stock.

WINE RECOMMENDATION

Salice Salentino, a rich and rustic red from southern Italy's Apulia, is a heartwarming match for this familiar classic. The wine is produced in vast quantities, making it a snap to find.

SERVES 4

¼ cup plus 4 teaspoons olive oil

1 onion, chopped

2 cloves garlic, minced

2 carrots, cut into ¼-inch dice

2 ribs celery, sliced

1 zucchini, cut in quarters lengthwise and then crosswise into thin slices

¾ pound green cabbage (about ¼ head), shredded (about 3 cups)

1½ quarts canned low-sodium chicken broth or homemade stock

1⅔ cups drained and rinsed canned pinto beans (one 15-ounce can)

½ cup arborio rice

¾ pound boiling potatoes (about 2), peeled and cut into ¼-inch dice

1 tablespoon tomato paste

1 bay leaf

½ teaspoon dried thyme

2¼ teaspoons salt

¼ teaspoon fresh-ground black pepper

2 tablespoons grated Parmesan

1. In a large pot, heat the ¼ cup oil over moderate heat. Add the onion and cook, stirring occasionally, until golden, about 10 minutes. Add the garlic, carrots, and celery. Cook, stirring occasionally, for 5 minutes. Add the zucchini and cabbage. Cook, stirring occasionally, until the vegetables start to soften, about 5 minutes longer.

2. Add the broth, beans, rice, potatoes, tomato paste, bay leaf, thyme, and salt to the pot. Bring to a boil. Reduce the heat and simmer, partially covered, until the rice and vegetables are tender, about 15 minutes. Remove the bay leaf.

3. Stir the pepper into the soup. Sprinkle each bowlful with Parmesan and drizzle each with 1 teaspoon of the remaining oil.

Risi e Bisi with Ham and Parmesan

A favorite of the rice-loving Venetians, the soup called *risi e bisi* (rice and peas) is so thick that it's sometimes mistaken for risotto. We've added diced ham and plenty of Parmesan to make a satisfying dinner.

WINE RECOMMENDATION

A light and unpretentious red will make the best partner for this dish. Look to the Veneto for the tart-cherry flavor of a crisp Bardolino or a slightly fuller Valpolicella.

SERVES 4

- 6 tablespoons butter
- 1 onion, chopped
- 1 rib celery, chopped
- 1 large clove garlic, minced
- ½ cup dry white wine
- 2 quarts canned low-sodium chicken broth or homemade stock
- 1½ cups rice, preferably arborio
- 2 tablespoons chopped fresh parsley
- 1¾ teaspoons salt
- 2 cups frozen petite peas (one 10-ounce package), defrosted
- 1 ¼-pound piece deli ham, cut into small dice
- ¾ cup grated Parmesan
- ½ teaspoon fresh-ground black pepper

1. In a large pot, melt the butter over moderately low heat. Add the onion, celery, and garlic and cook, stirring occasionally, until the vegetables start to soften, about 5 minutes. Add the wine and boil until it almost evaporates, about 5 minutes. Add the broth and bring to a boil. Boil until the liquid is reduced to approximately 7 cups, about 20 minutes.

2. Add the rice, parsley, and salt and cook at a low boil, stirring occasionally, until the rice is just tender, 10 to 15 minutes. Stir in the peas, ham, Parmesan, and pepper.

Petite Peas

Peas are one of the few vegetables that are usually better frozen than fresh. Frozen petite peas consistently have good flavor, a pleasant sweetness, and tender texture. In the springtime, if you can find truly fresh, sweet peas, by all means use them here. Just add them with the rice and parsley.

VENETIAN FISH SOUP

You can, and should, make this with whatever firm or moderately firm fish look best in the market. For a delicious traditional addition to the soup, toast four slices of good country-style bread and rub each piece with the cut-side of a halved garlic clove. Put a piece of toast in the bottom of each bowl and ladle the soup over it.

WINE RECOMMENDATION
Tomato-based fish dishes are just fine with red wine. Here, a refreshingly light and fruity Bardolino from the Veneto will be perfect.

SERVES 4

½ pound large shrimp, shells removed and reserved

2 cups water

3 tablespoons olive oil

2 carrots, chopped

2 onions, chopped

1 fennel bulb, chopped

2 ribs celery, chopped

6 cloves garlic, minced

½ cup dry white wine

3½ cups bottled clam juice

2½ cups canned crushed tomatoes in thick puree (from a 28-ounce can)

¼ teaspoon dried red-pepper flakes

5 tablespoons chopped fresh parsley

½ teaspoon dried thyme

1 teaspoon salt or more, depending on the saltiness of the clam juice

2 bay leaves

2 pounds moderately firm white fish fillets (use a mixture of 2 or 3 kinds), such as cod, halibut, ocean perch, orange roughy, pollack, red snapper, or tilapia, cut into 1-by-1-inch pieces

⅛ teaspoon fresh-ground black pepper

1. Put the shrimp shells and the water in a small pot; bring the water to a boil. Reduce the heat and simmer, covered, for 15 minutes. Strain the shrimp stock into a bowl. Discard the shells.

2. In a large pot, heat the oil over moderate heat. Add the carrots, onions, fennel, celery, and garlic; cook, stirring occasionally, until the vegetables start to soften, about 5 minutes. Add the wine; cook until it almost evaporates, about 5 minutes. Stir in the shrimp stock, clam juice, tomatoes, red-pepper flakes, 4 tablespoons of the parsley, the thyme, salt, and bay leaves. Bring to a boil. Reduce the heat and simmer, partially covered, for 25 minutes. Taste for salt and, if needed, add more. Remove the bay leaves.

3. Add the fish, shrimp, the remaining tablespoon parsley, and the pepper to the pot and bring to a simmer. Simmer until the fish and shrimp are just done, about 2 minutes.

ESCAROLE SOUP WITH CHICKEN AND RICE

Since the chicken is cut into such small pieces, it cooks in no time. Add it to the pot, simmer very briefly, and then serve the soup right away before the chicken has a chance to overcook.

WINE RECOMMENDATION

Avoid a red wine—its tannins will accentuate the bitterness of the greens. Instead, try a rich tocai friulano, the nuttiness of which will complement the escarole.

SERVES 4

- 3 tablespoons olive oil
- 1 carrot, chopped
- 1 onion, chopped
- 1 rib celery, chopped
- 4 cloves garlic, minced
- 7½ cups canned low-sodium chicken broth or homemade stock
- ¾ cup rice, preferably arborio
- 1½ teaspoons salt
- ¾ pound escarole (1 small head), leaves washed and cut into ½-inch ribbons
- 1⅓ pounds boneless, skinless chicken breasts (about 4 in all), cut into ½-inch dice
- ½ teaspoon fresh-ground black pepper
- 2 tablespoons chopped fresh parsley
- 6 tablespoons grated Parmesan

1. In a large pot, heat the oil over moderately low heat. Add the carrot, onion, celery, and garlic and cook, stirring occasionally, until the vegetables start to soften, about 5 minutes. Add the broth, rice, and salt. Bring to a boil. Reduce the heat and simmer, partially covered, for 10 minutes.

2. Add the escarole to the pot. Bring to a simmer and cook until the escarole is almost tender, about 5 minutes. Add the chicken and pepper. Bring to a simmer and continue simmering for just 1 minute. The chicken should be done.

3. Remove the pot from the heat. Stir in the parsley and Parmesan.

VARIATION

For a richer soup, stir two well-beaten **eggs** into the pot along with the parsley and Parmesan cheese (after removing the pot from the heat).

SPLIT-PEA SOUP WITH PORTOBELLOS

Meaty portobellos are especially good for adding substance and flavor to this soup, but shiitakes or other mushrooms will work well, too. You can also add a ham hock to the pot while the split peas cook, if you like.

WINE RECOMMENDATION

You'll need a white wine with body and lots of character to stand up to a hearty pea soup like this one. Greco di Tufo, with its full texture and big, nutty taste, is made for the job.

SERVES 4

4 tablespoons olive oil

2 carrots, chopped

2 onions, chopped

2 ribs celery, chopped

3 cloves garlic, minced

1⅔ cups green split peas

3 tablespoons chopped fresh parsley

9 cups water

½ teaspoon dried thyme

1 bay leaf

2 teaspoons salt

1 pound portobello mushrooms, stems removed, caps cut into ½-inch dice

6 tablespoons grated Parmesan

¼ teaspoon fresh-ground black pepper

1. In a large pot, heat 2 tablespoons of the oil over moderate heat. Add the carrots, onions, celery, and garlic. Cook, stirring occasionally, until the vegetables start to soften, about 5 minutes.

2. Add the split peas, parsley, water, thyme, and bay leaf. Bring to a boil. Reduce the heat and cook at a low boil, covered, until the peas are almost tender, about 35 minutes. Add 1¾ teaspoons of the salt and simmer 5 minutes longer. Remove the bay leaf.

3. Meanwhile, in a large nonstick frying pan, heat the remaining 2 tablespoons oil over moderately high heat. Add the mushrooms and the remaining ¼ teaspoon salt. Cook until the mushrooms brown, 5 to 10 minutes. Add the mushrooms to the soup and bring back to a simmer. Stir in the Parmesan and pepper.

LENTIL SOUP WITH TUBETTI AND BACON

Vegetables, lentils, and pasta simmer in a broth. The soup is infused with the earthy flavors of bacon and rosemary. We use tubetti, but any small macaroni shape will work as well.

WINE RECOMMENDATION
The nebbiolo grape produces wine with complex notes including smoke, truffle, and dried red cherry. A light-bodied version, such as one from Valtellina, is an excellent match.

SERVES 4

¼	pound bacon, slices cut crosswise into ½-inch strips
2	carrots, cut into 1-inch pieces
2	onions, cut into 1-inch chunks
2	ribs celery, cut into 1-inch pieces
½	pound mushrooms, sliced
6	cloves garlic, peeled
1	pound lentils (about 2⅓ cups)
1½	quarts canned low-sodium chicken broth or homemade stock
3	cups water
1	teaspoon dried rosemary, or 1 tablespoon chopped fresh rosemary
1	cup canned tomatoes in thick puree, chopped
2	teaspoons salt
¼	teaspoon dried red-pepper flakes
¼	teaspoon fresh-ground black pepper
½	cup tubetti or other small macaroni

1. In a large pot, cook the bacon over moderate heat until crisp. Remove. Pour off all but 2 tablespoons of the fat. Add the carrots, onions, celery, mushrooms, and garlic. Cook, stirring occasionally, until the vegetables start to soften, about 5 minutes.

2. Add the lentils, broth, water, rosemary, tomatoes, salt, red-pepper flakes, black pepper, and bacon. Bring to a boil. Reduce the heat and simmer for 15 minutes. Add the pasta and simmer until the lentils are tender and the pasta is done, 10 to 15 minutes longer.

VARIATIONS

■ Substitute an equal amount of **pancetta** for the bacon.
■ Use **thyme** instead of rosemary.
■ Add shredded **spinach** or **escarole** leaves during the last few minutes of cooking.

CHICKPEA SOUP WITH SWISS CHARD

The humble chickpea is enormously popular in Italy, especially for soups. Here, in this Tuscan specialty, it's joined by tomatoes, macaroni, Swiss-chard leaves, and a generous quantity of garlic.

WINE RECOMMENDATION
Since a red wine would accent the Swiss chard's bitterness, try a full-bodied tocai friulano. Its nutty flavor will mirror that of the chickpeas.

SERVES 4

6   cups drained and rinsed canned chickpeas (three 19-ounce cans)

3   cups canned low-sodium chicken broth or homemade stock, more if needed

3   tablespoons olive oil

1   carrot, chopped

1   onion, chopped

1   rib celery, chopped

4   cloves garlic, minced

1   teaspoon dried rosemary, or 1 tablespoon chopped fresh rosemary

1   bay leaf

    Pinch dried red-pepper flakes

1   cup canned tomatoes in thick puree, chopped

½   cup tubetti or other small macaroni

1   teaspoon salt

½   pound Swiss chard, tough stems removed, leaves cut into 1-inch pieces

¼   teaspoon fresh-ground black pepper

1. Puree half of the chickpeas with 1½ cups of the broth in a blender or food processor. In a large pot, heat the oil over moderately low heat. Add the carrot, onion, celery, garlic, and rosemary and cook, stirring occasionally, until the vegetables start to soften, about 5 minutes.

2. Stir in the remaining 1½ cups broth, the pureed chickpeas, whole chickpeas, bay leaf, red-pepper flakes, tomatoes, tubetti, and salt. Bring to a boil. Reduce the heat and simmer, partially covered, for 10 minutes.

3. Add the Swiss chard to the pot. Simmer until the chard is tender and the pasta is done, 5 to 10 minutes longer. Remove the bay leaf. Stir in the black pepper. If the soup thickens too much on standing, stir in more broth or water.

PASTA E FAGIOLI WITH SAUSAGE

The much-beloved *pasta e fagioli* (pasta and beans), adorned here with sliced sausage, is truly a meal in itself. The soup has very little liquid and will thicken as it sits. If you'd like to thin it a bit, add a little more chicken broth or water.

WINE RECOMMENDATION
This hearty favorite is best accompanied by a light, sprightly grignolino. Almost more rosé than red wine, grignolino has a penetrating floral aroma and spicy flavor.

SERVES 4

- 2 tablespoons olive oil
- 1 pound mild Italian sausages
- 1 carrot, chopped fine
- 1 onion, chopped fine
- 1 rib celery, chopped fine
- 4 cloves garlic, minced
- 1 teaspoon dried rosemary, or 1 tablespoon chopped fresh rosemary
- 6 cups drained and rinsed canned kidney beans (three 19-ounce cans)
- 2¾ cups canned low-sodium chicken broth or homemade stock
- 1 bay leaf
- 1 teaspoon salt
- ½ cup tubetti or other small macaroni
- ½ teaspoon fresh-ground black pepper

1. In a large pot, heat 1 tablespoon of the oil over moderate heat. Add the sausages and cook, turning, until browned and cooked through, about 10 minutes. Remove. When cool enough to handle, halve the sausages lengthwise and then cut crosswise into slices.

2. Heat the remaining tablespoon of oil in the pot over moderately low heat. Add the carrot, onion, celery, garlic, and rosemary. Cook, stirring occasionally, until the vegetables start to soften, about 10 minutes.

3. Puree 4 cups of the beans with 1¼ cups of the broth in a blender or food processor. Add the puree to the pot along with the remaining 1½ cups broth, the whole beans, bay leaf, and salt. Bring to a boil. Reduce the heat and simmer, partially covered, for 15 minutes.

4. Stir in the pasta. Cook the soup over moderate heat, partially covered, stirring frequently, until the pasta is done, 10 to 15 minutes. Remove the bay leaf. Stir in the sausage and the pepper. Cook until the sausage is warmed through, about 1 minute.

SAUSAGE AND MUSHROOM SOUP

Strands of angel-hair pasta form a web in the broth, capturing the slices of sausage and mushroom. Red-pepper flakes give the soup its spiciness; to turn up the heat another notch, use hot Italian sausage instead of mild.

WINE RECOMMENDATION
A Valtellina from northern Piedmont will nicely echo the earthy mushroom and spicy sausage flavors here. The wine is made from the nebbiolo grape, as are the more familiar Barolo and Barbaresco.

SERVES 4

2	tablespoons olive oil
1¼	pounds mild Italian sausages
1	onion, chopped
3	cloves garlic, minced
1	pound mushrooms, sliced
7	cups canned low-sodium chicken broth or homemade stock
½	teaspoon dried thyme
¼	teaspoon dried red-pepper flakes
4	tablespoons chopped fresh parsley
1¾	teaspoons salt
¼	pound angel hair
⅛	teaspoon fresh-ground black pepper

1. In a large pot, heat 1 tablespoon of the oil over moderate heat. Add the sausages and cook, turning occasionally, until browned and cooked through, about 10 minutes. Remove.

When cool enough to handle, cut the sausages into ⅛-inch slices.

2. Heat the remaining 1 tablespoon oil in the pot over moderately low heat. Add the onion and garlic and cook, stirring occasionally, until the onion is translucent, about 5 minutes. Add the mushrooms and cook until golden, 5 to 10 minutes.

3. Add the broth, thyme, red-pepper flakes, 2 tablespoons of the parsley, and the salt to the pot. Bring to a boil. Reduce the heat and simmer, partially covered, for 15 minutes. Stir in the sausages and bring back to a boil. Add the pasta, reduce the heat, and simmer until just done, about 3 minutes. Stir in the remaining 2 tablespoons parsley and the black pepper.

SICILIAN MEATBALL SOUP

Flavored with Parmesan and garlic and studded with raisins, scrumptious Sicilian meatballs turn vegetable soup into a tempting meal. If the soup waits, the pasta may absorb much of the liquid; just add water or more stock.

WINE RECOMMENDATION
This robust potion calls for a similarly rustic southern red. Look for Corvo, a smooth and satisfying wine from the well-known firm Duca di Salaparuta.

SERVES 4

½ pound ground beef

5 tablespoons chopped fresh parsley

¼ cup grated Parmesan, plus more for serving

2 tablespoons raisins

2 tablespoons dry bread crumbs

1 egg, beaten

5 cloves garlic, minced

2½ teaspoons salt

½ teaspoon fresh-ground black pepper

2 tablespoons olive oil

2 carrots, cut into ¼-inch dice

1 onion, chopped

2 ribs celery, cut into ¼-inch dice

1 zucchini, cut into ¼-inch dice

1½ quarts canned low-sodium chicken broth or homemade stock

1 cup canned crushed tomatoes in thick puree

½ teaspoon dried rosemary, or 2 teaspoons chopped fresh rosemary

1 cup small pasta shells or other small macaroni

1. In a medium bowl, mix together the ground beef, 4 tablespoons of the parsley, the Parmesan, raisins, bread crumbs, egg, half of the garlic, ½ teaspoon of the salt, and ¼ teaspoon of the pepper until thoroughly combined. Shape the mixture into 24 meatballs.

2. In a large pot, heat the oil over moderate heat. Add the carrots, onion, celery, and the remaining garlic and cook, stirring occasionally, until the vegetables start to soften, about 5 minutes. Add the zucchini and cook, stirring occasionally, for 5 minutes. Stir in the broth, tomatoes, rosemary, and the remaining 2 teaspoons salt. Bring to a boil. Reduce the heat and simmer, partially covered, for 10 minutes.

3. Add the remaining tablespoon parsley, ¼ teaspoon pepper, and the pasta to the soup. Simmer for 5 minutes. Stir in the meatballs and simmer gently until the meatballs and pasta are done, about 5 minutes longer. Serve with additional Parmesan.

CHAPTER THREE

Pasta

FUSILLI WITH ZUCCHINI AND FONDUTA

The classic Piedmontese *fonduta* combines fontina cheese, milk, egg yolks, and butter into a silky sauce that's usually topped with thin slices of white truffle. Traditionally, *fonduta* is served with toast or fried polenta. Our version (minus the truffle) coats fusilli and strips of zucchini for a divine rendition of macaroni and cheese.

WINE RECOMMENDATION
Do not try to match this dish's richness; go for contrast instead. Piedmont's own Nebbiolo della Langhe, a spicy, earthy red wine with subtle hints of truffle, is what you want.

SERVES 4

¾ pound fontina, grated (about 3 cups)

1¼ cups milk

3 egg yolks

3 tablespoons butter, cut into pieces, at room temperature

1¼ teaspoons salt

½ teaspoon fresh-ground black pepper

1 pound fusilli

4 zucchini (about 1½ pounds), seeded and cut into ¼-by-2-inch matchstick strips

1. In a medium heatproof bowl, combine the grated cheese and the milk. Allow the mixture to stand for 20 minutes and then drain off the milk, reserving ¼ cup. Set the bowl with the cheese over a saucepan of barely simmering water, or transfer the cheese to the top of a double boiler. Whisk until the cheese melts, about 5 minutes.

2. In a small bowl, whisk together the egg yolks and the reserved ¼ cup milk and add to the melted cheese with the butter, whisking. The mixture will separate. Add the salt and pepper and continue whisking until the sauce is almost smooth, about 3 minutes longer. Do not cook too long or the mixture will curdle. The sauce will not be completely smooth.

3. Meanwhile, in a large pot of boiling, salted water, cook the fusilli for 10 minutes. Add the zucchini and bring back to a boil. Cook until the zucchini and pasta are just done, about 3 minutes longer. Drain. Toss with the *fonduta*.

SEEDING ZUCCHINI

Because the zucchini are boiled here, we recommend seeding them first; otherwise, the pulpy seeds become water-logged. To remove the seeds, cut the zucchini into quarters lengthwise. Then simply cut off the seeds.

Spaghetti with Tomatoes, Basil, Olives, and Fresh Mozzarella

Since the tomatoes here are not cooked, you'll really notice their flavor—or lack of it. Make this sauce in the summer when fresh tomatoes are at their peak. The garlic is heated briefly in the oil, and then the garlicky oil is tossed with the spaghetti so the flavor is dispersed throughout the dish. The pasta is equally good warm and at room temperature.

WINE RECOMMENDATION

Valpolicella, the crisp, fruity, cherry-scented wine from the shores of Lake Garda in the Veneto, is the perfect hot-weather wine for tomato-and-herb-based dishes. Try one here for a delightful accompaniment.

SERVES 4

- 2 pounds vine-ripened tomatoes (about 6), chopped
- ¾ pound salted fresh mozzarella, cut into ¼-inch cubes, at room temperature
- 1¼ cups chopped fresh basil
- ½ cup halved and pitted black olives
- 4 teaspoons balsamic vinegar
- 1¼ teaspoons salt
- ½ teaspoon fresh-ground black pepper
- 1 pound spaghetti
- ½ cup olive oil
- 3 cloves garlic, minced

1. In a large glass or stainless-steel bowl, combine the chopped tomatoes with the mozzarella, basil, olives, balsamic vinegar, salt, and pepper.

2. In a large pot of boiling, salted water, cook the spaghetti until just done, about 12 minutes. Drain, add to the tomato mixture, and toss.

3. Heat the oil in a small frying pan over moderately low heat. Add the garlic and cook, stirring, for 1 minute. Pour the oil over the pasta and toss again.

VARIATIONS

Add some drained **capers**, chopped **red onion**, or grated **Parmesan** to the pasta.

ZITI, EGGPLANT, AND FONTINA GRATIN

Eggplant is sautéed in olive oil until it's creamy soft and then tossed with pasta and cheese. A quick stint under the broiler melts the fontina and browns the top.

WINE RECOMMENDATION
Though *dolcetto* translates as little sweet one, that refers to the grape; the wine is delightfully dry. It will make an ideal partner for this tasty dish.

SERVES 4

7   tablespoons olive oil

1   large eggplant (about 1¾ pounds), peeled and cut into ¼-inch dice

1¼   teaspoons salt

2   cloves garlic, minced

3   tablespoons chopped fresh parsley

½   teaspoon fresh-ground black pepper

1   pound ziti or penne

½   pound fontina, grated (about 2 cups)

1. In a large nonstick frying pan, heat 4 tablespoons of the oil over moderately high heat. Add the eggplant and ¾ teaspoon of the salt and cook, stirring frequently, until the eggplant is soft, 10 to 15 minutes. Stir in the garlic, parsley, and ¼ teaspoon of the pepper and cook 3 minutes longer.

2. Heat the broiler. In a large pot of boiling, salted water, cook the pasta until just done, about 10 to 15 minutes. Drain.

3. Toss the pasta with the eggplant, the remaining 3 tablespoons oil, ½ teaspoon salt, and ¼ teaspoon pepper. Add the cheese and toss again. Transfer the pasta to a shallow baking dish or gratin dish. Broil until the cheese melts and starts to brown, 2 to 3 minutes.

EGGPLANT CONTROVERSIES

■ Cooks in Italy, as everywhere, disagree about whether or not eggplant should be peeled. It seems to be a matter of personal preference, but keep in mind that an eggplant that is overgrown or has been stored for a long time will have a tough skin that will not soften during cooking. It's often a good idea to peel it.

■ Whether or not to salt and drain eggplant before cooking remains a matter of dispute, too. Some say you should salt slices heavily and drain them on paper towels for an hour to rid the eggplant of any bitterness; others feel it's an unnecessary step. What is indisputably true is that eggplant that has been salted and drained will absorb less oil during frying than eggplant that has not.

LINGUINE WITH CAULIFLOWER, GARLIC, AND BREAD CRUMBS

The strong flavors of cauliflower, garlic, red-pepper flakes, and Parmesan cheese balance perfectly, raising these common, readily available ingredients to new heights.

WINE RECOMMENDATION
Red wine, if it's simple and crisp, makes an intriguing choice for this dish. A touch of earthiness, such as you'll find in a basic Chianti, helps to tie the wine and food flavors together.

SERVES 4

  8 tablespoons olive oil

  1 cup fresh bread crumbs

  6 cloves garlic, minced

  6 tablespoons chopped fresh parsley

  ½ teaspoon dried red-pepper flakes

  1 teaspoon anchovy paste

  1 pound linguine

  1 head cauliflower (about 2½ pounds), cut into small florets

  1 teaspoon salt

  ½ cup grated Parmesan, plus more for serving

1. In a large frying pan, heat 4 tablespoons of the oil over moderate heat. Add the bread crumbs and cook, stirring, until golden, about 5 minutes. Remove. Wipe out the pan.

2. Heat the remaining 4 tablespoons oil in the same pan over moderately low heat. Add the garlic, parsley, and red-pepper flakes. Cook, stirring, for 1 minute. Stir in the anchovy paste. Remove from the heat.

3. In a large pot of boiling, salted water, cook the linguine until almost done, about 8 minutes. Add the cauliflower and bring back to a boil. Cook until the cauliflower and pasta are just done, about 4 minutes longer. Drain. Toss with the garlic mixture, salt, bread crumbs, and Parmesan. Top with additional Parmesan.

VARIATIONS

■ Substitute **broccoli** for the cauliflower.

■ Add a handful each of **raisins** and **pine nuts** at the same time as the garlic, parsley, and red-pepper flakes.

■ Use four chopped **anchovy fillets** instead of the anchovy paste.

Fettuccine with Gorgonzola and Broccoli

The very mention of Gorgonzola sets the taste buds tingling, and this smooth, sublime sauce doesn't disappoint. We made the pasta with broccoli florets, but the stems are at least as good. If you prefer, buy half the quantity of broccoli; then peel the thick stems and cut them into eighth-inch rounds so they'll cook in the same time as the tops.

WINE RECOMMENDATION
Strong-flavored broccoli and Gorgonzola are a challenge to match with wine. A Fiano di Avellino's intense taste can take them on, and its acidity will cut the unctuousness of the sauce.

SERVES 4

- ¾ cup canned low-sodium chicken broth or homemade stock
- ½ cup dry white wine
- ½ pound Gorgonzola or other blue cheese, crumbled (about 2 cups)
- 2 cups heavy cream
- 3 tablespoons butter
- 1 teaspoon salt
- ¼ teaspoon fresh-ground black pepper
- 1 pound fettuccine
- 1¼ pounds broccoli (about 2 stalks), thick stems removed, tops cut into small florets (about 5 cups)
- ⅓ cup grated Parmesan, plus more for serving
- 3 tablespoons chopped fresh parsley

1. In a medium stainless-steel pot, combine the broth and wine and bring to a boil over moderate heat. Cook until the mixture is reduced to about ⅔ cup, 5 to 10 minutes.

2. Reduce the heat to moderately low and add the Gorgonzola, cream, and butter. Bring to a simmer; cook, stirring, until the cheese melts and the sauce thickens slightly, about 5 minutes. Add the salt and pepper. Remove from the heat.

3. In a large pot of boiling, salted water, cook the pasta until almost done, about 9 minutes. Add the broccoli florets and bring back to a boil. Cook until the broccoli and pasta are just done, about 3 minutes longer. Drain.

4. Toss the fettuccine and broccoli with the Gorgonzola sauce, Parmesan, and parsley. Serve with extra Parmesan.

Variations

Try the sauce and pasta with **asparagus**, **green beans**, or just **fresh herbs** instead of the broccoli.

PENNE ARRABBIATA WITH FLAKED COD

Arrabbiata means angry and is often used to describe a spicy tomato sauce. Cook the cod directly in the sauce and then break it into flakes. If you prefer, you can use another fish with large flakes, such as orange roughy or haddock, instead of the cod.

WINE RECOMMENDATION
The adage is white wine with fish, but the tomatoes in this sauce call for a red instead. Try a sprightly Lago di Caldero or an easier-to-find Valpolicella.

SERVES 4

¼ cup olive oil

2 cloves garlic, minced

3 cups canned crushed tomatoes in thick puree (one 28-ounce can)

1 large tomato, peeled and chopped

1¾ teaspoons salt

½ teaspoon dried red-pepper flakes

1 pound cod fillet, cut into 1-inch chunks

3 tablespoons chopped fresh parsley

1 pound penne

1. In a large saucepan, heat the oil over moderate heat. Add the garlic and cook, stirring, for 1 minute. Add the canned tomatoes, fresh tomato, salt, and red-pepper flakes and bring to a simmer. Simmer the sauce until thick, about 30 minutes.

2. Add the cod and 2 tablespoons of the parsley to the sauce. Bring back to a simmer and continue simmering until the fish is just done, 1 to 2 minutes. Break the fish into small pieces with a spoon.

3. Meanwhile, in a large pot of boiling, salted water, cook the penne until just done, about 13 minutes. Drain. Toss with the sauce. Top the pasta with the remaining tablespoon parsley.

VARIATION

To make this dish without a trip to the fish market, substitute two six-ounce cans of drained **tuna** for the cod. Stir it into the tomato sauce and warm for about a minute before tossing with the pasta.

TEST-KITCHEN TIP

To peel the fresh tomato quickly, make double use of the pasta-cooking water. Bring a pot of water to a boil, core the tomato, and drop it into the water for fifteen seconds. Using a slotted spoon, remove the tomato from the water, peel, and chop it. Then you've got boiling water ready for the pasta.

LINGUINE WITH TUNA, WALNUTS, LEMON, AND HERBS

Keep tuna on hand for quick, last-minute pasta sauces. Lemon zest, lemon juice, and tons of fresh herbs brighten this one. Though Italian cooks stick to canned tuna for this kind of sauce, you might try it with fresh tuna steaks, seared and sliced.

WINE RECOMMENDATION
Wines of Italy's Alto Adige show a strong Germanic influence due to the region's proximity to Switzerland. Try a flowery, lime-scented Müller-Thurgau for a refreshing change from the ordinary.

SERVES 4

¾ cup walnuts, chopped

1 pound linguine

⅓ cup olive oil

4 cloves garlic, minced

2 6-ounce cans tuna packed in oil

2 teaspoons grated lemon zest (from 2 lemons)

2 teaspoons lemon juice

¾ teaspoon salt

½ teaspoon fresh-ground black pepper

½ cup mixed chopped fresh herbs, such as parsley, chives, and thyme

1. In a small frying pan, toast the walnuts over moderately low heat, stirring frequently, until golden brown, about 5 minutes. Or toast them in a 350° oven for 5 to 10 minutes.

2. In a large pot of boiling, salted water, cook the linguine until just done, about 12 minutes. Drain.

3. Meanwhile, in a large frying pan, heat the olive oil over moderate heat. Add the garlic and cook, stirring, for 1 minute. Stir in the tuna and its oil and break up the tuna with a fork. Remove from the heat. Toss the linguine with the tuna mixture, the lemon zest, lemon juice, salt, pepper, herbs, and the toasted walnuts.

CANNED TUNA

Brands of tuna vary tremendously. Here we use tuna packed in oil (preferably olive oil), and we count on that oil as part of the sauce. If your tuna has less than one and a half tablespoons oil per can, add more olive oil to make up the difference.

Pasta con le Sarde

If you've never been a fan of sardines, this recipe may be the key to your conversion. Italians rarely combine fish with cheese, but here we've mixed grated Parmesan with the crisp bread crumbs for a topping too delectable to leave out.

WINE RECOMMENDATION
Mastroberardino is the acknowledged master winemaker of southern Italy. His Lacrimarosa, a uniquely earthy, tart, and delicately flavored rosé, seems to have been made with a dish such as this in mind.

SERVES 4

½	cup olive oil
1	cup fresh bread crumbs
½	cup grated Parmesan
1	fennel bulb, diced
4	cloves garlic, minced
1	cup canned crushed tomatoes in thick puree
2	4⅜-ounce cans boneless and skinless sardines, drained
¼	cup chopped fresh parsley
¾	teaspoon salt
½	teaspoon fresh-ground black pepper
1	pound spaghetti

1. In a large frying pan, heat ¼ cup of the oil over moderate heat. Add the bread crumbs and cook, stirring, until golden, about 5 minutes. Remove the crumbs from the pan and toss with the Parmesan. Wipe out the pan.

2. In the same pan, heat the remaining ¼ cup oil over moderately high heat. Add the fennel and cook, stirring occasionally, until golden, 5 to 10 minutes. Add the garlic and cook, stirring, 1 minute longer. Stir in the tomatoes and bring to a simmer. Reduce the heat and simmer until thick, about 10 minutes. Add the sardines, parsley, salt, and pepper. Break up the sardines with a fork. Remove from the heat.

3. In a large pot of boiling, salted water, cook the spaghetti until just done, about 12 minutes. Drain. Toss the spaghetti with the sauce and half of the bread crumbs. Top with the remaining crumbs.

Variation

If you're fortunate enough to find fresh **sardines**, substitute one pound of them, filleted, for the canned sardines. Add them to the pan along with the garlic and sauté for two to three minutes before adding the tomatoes.

FARFALLE WITH PROSCIUTTO, SPINACH, PINE NUTS, AND RAISINS

The farfalle act like little shovels scooping up the pine nuts and raisins. Another pasta with the same facility, such as shells, will work equally well. Prosciutto and Parmesan add piquancy and saltiness to the dish, perfectly complementing the sweet raisins.

WINE RECOMMENDATION
A fragrant and spicy gewürztraminer from the Alto Adige makes an unlikely but tasty mate for this pasta.

SERVES 4

½ cup pine nuts

½ cup raisins

½ cup boiling water

½ cup olive oil

6 cloves garlic, minced

10 ounces spinach, large stems removed, leaves washed and cut crosswise into 1-inch strips

1 pound farfalle

¼ pound sliced prosciutto, cut crosswise into ¼-inch strips

½ teaspoon salt

½ teaspoon fresh-ground black pepper

⅓ cup grated Parmesan

1. In a small frying pan, toast the pine nuts over moderately low heat, stirring frequently, until golden brown, about 5 minutes. Or toast them in a 350° oven for 5 to 10 minutes.

2. Combine the raisins and the boiling water. Let stand until plump, about 10 minutes. Drain.

3. In a large frying pan, heat the oil over moderately low heat. Add the garlic and cook, stirring, for 1 minute. Stir in the spinach and cook, stirring, until just wilted, about 2 minutes.

4. In a large pot of boiling, salted water, cook the farfalle until just done, about 15 minutes. Drain. Toss with the pine nuts, raisins, spinach mixture, prosciutto, salt, pepper, and Parmesan.

VARIATIONS

- Replace the pine nuts with **walnuts**.
- Substitute **Swiss chard** for the spinach.

ORECCHIETTE WITH BROCCOLI RABE, BACON, AND BREAD CRUMBS

For a pleasant change of pace, we toss crisp, golden bread crumbs with the pasta instead of the usual grated cheese. If you don't have orecchiette, replace them with shells, bow ties, rotelle, or fusilli.

WINE RECOMMENDATION

The bitter bite of the broccoli rabe and the pungent garlic in this dish both require a crisp white wine to act as a neutral foil. Try a pinot grigio from Friuli for good effect.

SERVES 4

- 1 pound broccoli rabe, tough ends removed, cut into 1-inch lengths
- ½ cup olive oil
- 1 cup fresh bread crumbs
- 4 slices bacon, cut crosswise into ¼-inch strips
- 6 cloves garlic, minced
- ¼ teaspoon dried red-pepper flakes
- 1 pound orecchiette
- ¾ teaspoon salt

1. In a medium pot of boiling, salted water, cook the broccoli rabe until almost done, about 3 minutes. Drain thoroughly.

2. In a large nonstick frying pan, heat ¼ cup of the oil over moderate heat. Add the bread crumbs and cook, stirring, until golden, about 5 minutes. Remove. Wipe out the pan.

3. In the same pan, cook the bacon until crisp. Remove the bacon and drain on paper towels. Pour off all the fat. Heat the remaining ¼ cup oil in the frying pan over moderately low heat. Add the garlic and red-pepper flakes and cook, stirring, for 1 minute. Add the broccoli rabe and cook, stirring occasionally, until just done, about 3 minutes longer.

4. In a large pot of boiling, salted water, cook the orecchiette until done, about 15 minutes. Drain and toss with the bread crumbs, bacon, broccoli rabe, and salt.

FRESH BREAD CRUMBS

The quickest way to make fresh bread crumbs is to tear up a few slices of French or Italian bread and whir them in the food processor. No need to remove the crust.

Cavatelli with Sardinian Meat Sauce

Frozen cavatelli is better than dried. Since this shape is thick and doughy, the dried version tends to get overcooked on the outside before it's done inside. If you can't find cavatelli in the freezer section of your grocery store, a chunky dried pasta such as rigatoni will also be excellent here. Use the same quantity.

WINE RECOMMENDATION
Red wines from Sardinia are almost impossible to find in the U.S., but a sturdy Cirò, made across the water in Calabria from the gaglioppo grapes, will be a fine substitute.

SERVES 4

3 tablespoons olive oil

¾ pound hot Italian sausage, casings removed

1 onion, chopped

3 cloves garlic, minced

3 cups canned crushed tomatoes in thick puree (one 28-ounce can)

3 tablespoons chopped fresh mint (optional)

⅓ cup chopped fresh parsley

¼ cup water

1¼ teaspoons salt

2 large pinches saffron (optional)

1 pound frozen cavatelli

¼ cup chopped fresh basil

3 tablespoons grated Pecorino Romano or Parmesan, plus more for serving

1. In a large deep frying pan or Dutch oven, heat 1 tablespoon of the oil over moderate heat. Add the sausage and cook, breaking up the meat with a fork, until it is no longer pink, about 5 minutes.

2. Reduce the heat to moderately low and add the remaining 2 tablespoons oil to the pan. Stir in the onion and garlic. Cook, stirring occasionally, until the onion is translucent, about 5 minutes. Add the tomatoes, mint, parsley, water, salt, and 1 pinch of the saffron. Simmer until thickened, about 15 minutes.

3. Meanwhile, in a large pot of boiling salted water, cook the cavatelli with the remaining pinch saffron until just done, 10 to 15 minutes. Reserve ½ cup of the pasta water. Drain the cavatelli and toss with the meat sauce, the basil, the reserved pasta water, and the cheese. Serve with additional Pecorino Romano.

Sausage Substitutes

If you can't find hot Italian sausage, use ground pork or mild sausage and a quarter teaspoon of dried red-pepper flakes.

RIGATONI WITH SAUSAGE AND TOMATO CREAM SAUCE

Tubes of rigatoni hold the tomato sauce, giving you a burst of creamy flavor with every bite. Use either hot or mild Italian sausage here, depending on your preference.

WINE RECOMMENDATION
A Chianti Classico Riserva is the wine of choice with this dish. Look for a wine with a few years of age; it will be mellower and will complement the sauce better than a younger wine could.

SERVES 4

1 tablespoon olive oil

1½ pounds mild or hot Italian sausage, casings removed

1 onion, chopped

3 cloves garlic, minced

⅓ cup dry white wine

1½ cups canned crushed tomatoes in thick puree (from a 15-ounce can)

½ teaspoon salt

½ teaspoon fresh-ground black pepper

¼ cup chopped fresh parsley

1 cup light cream

1 pound rigatoni

Grated Parmesan, for serving

1. In a large frying pan, heat the oil over moderate heat. Add the sausage and cook, breaking up the meat with a fork, until it is no longer pink, about 5 minutes. With a slotted spoon, remove the sausage from the pan. Discard all but 1 tablespoon fat.

2. Reduce the heat to moderately low. Add the onion and garlic and cook, stirring occasionally, until the onion is translucent, about 5 minutes. Add the wine and cook until it almost evaporates, about 5 minutes. Stir in the sausage, tomatoes, and salt. Simmer, covered, for 10 minutes. Add the pepper, parsley, and cream.

3. In a large pot of boiling, salted water, cook the rigatoni until just done, about 14 minutes. Drain the pasta and toss with the sauce. Serve with grated Parmesan.

CHAPTER FOUR

Rice
&
Polenta

SUN-DRIED-TOMATO AND PESTO RISOTTO

Even if the sun-dried tomatoes are dry-packed, there's no need to soak them before adding them to the risotto; the simmering broth will reconstitute them as the rice cooks. The pesto, along with the tomatoes, makes this an especially flavorful dish.

WINE RECOMMENDATION
Go for a vibrant sauvignon blanc from the Collio district of Friuli. The herbal components of the wine will mesh beautifully with the pesto in the risotto.

SERVES 4

5 cups canned low-sodium chicken broth or homemade stock, more if needed

1 cup water, more if needed

3 tablespoons olive oil

1 onion, chopped

2 cups arborio rice

½ cup dry white wine

1¼ teaspoons salt

½ cup dry-packed or oil-packed sun-dried tomatoes, chopped

¼ teaspoon fresh-ground black pepper

3 tablespoons store-bought or homemade pesto

¼ cup grated Parmesan, more for serving

1. In a medium saucepan, bring the broth and water to a simmer. In a large pot, heat the oil over moderately low heat. Add the onion and cook, stirring occasionally, until translucent, about 5 minutes.

2. Add the rice to the pot and stir until it begins to turn opaque, about 2 minutes. Add the wine and salt and cook, stirring frequently, until all the wine has been absorbed.

3. Add the sun-dried tomatoes and about ½ cup of the simmering broth to the rice and cook, stirring frequently, until the broth has been completely absorbed. The rice and broth should bubble gently; adjust the heat as needed. Continue cooking the rice, adding broth ½ cup at a time and allowing the rice to absorb the broth before adding the next ½ cup. Cook the rice in this way until tender, 25 to 30 minutes in all. The broth that hasn't been absorbed should be thickened by the starch from the rice. You may not need to use all of the liquid, or you may need more broth or some water.

4. Stir in the pepper, pesto, and Parmesan. Serve the risotto with additional Parmesan.

RISOTTO WITH RADICCHIO AND SMOKED MOZZARELLA

Mellow, melting cubes of smoked mozzarella balance the slightly bitter radicchio perfectly. You can use curly endive in place of the radicchio, if you prefer, or escarole if you want to eliminate the bitterness. Substitute salted mozzarella if smoked is not available.

WINE RECOMMENDATION
Here's a risotto that can stand up to red wine. Try an unoaked Barbera d'Alba, a lively and fruity wine whose very light tannins won't accentuate the bitterness of the radicchio.

SERVES 4

  5 cups canned low-sodium chicken broth or homemade stock, more if needed

  1 cup water, more if needed

  2 tablespoons olive oil

  1 onion, chopped

  2 cups arborio rice

  ½ cup dry white wine

1¾ teaspoons salt

  1 head radicchio (about ½ pound), cut into 1-inch pieces

  3 tablespoons chopped fresh parsley

  ¼ teaspoon fresh-ground black pepper

  2 tablespoons butter

  ½ pound smoked mozzarella, cut into ¼-inch dice

1. In a medium saucepan, bring the broth and water to a simmer. In a large pot, heat the oil over moderately low heat. Add the onion and cook, stirring occasionally, until translucent, about 5 minutes.

2. Add the rice to the pot and stir until it begins to turn opaque, about 2 minutes. Add the wine and salt and cook, stirring frequently, until all the wine has been absorbed.

3. Add about ½ cup of the simmering broth to the rice and cook, stirring frequently, until the broth has been completely absorbed. The rice and broth should bubble gently; adjust the heat as needed. Continue cooking the rice, adding broth ½ cup at a time and allowing the rice to absorb the broth before adding the next ½ cup. Cook the rice in this way until almost tender, about 20 minutes. Add the radicchio and parsley and cook until the radicchio and the rice are tender, about 5 minutes more. The broth that hasn't been absorbed should be thickened by the starch from the rice. You may not need to use all of the liquid, or you may need more broth or some water.

4. Stir the pepper and the butter into the risotto. Add the mozzarella and stir until it melts into a web.

DRIED-PORCINI-MUSHROOM RISOTTO WITH GOAT CHEESE

Using the mushroom-soaking liquid to cook the rice gives this risotto intense flavor. There's just enough goat cheese to balance the earthiness of the porcini with a touch of tartness without overwhelming the dish.

WINE RECOMMENDATION
Tuscany's chardonnays, loaded with tropical-fruit flavors and generously oaked, are not typically Italian. No matter; they have the power and concentration to make a great combination here.

SERVES 4

- 1 cup dried porcini or other dried mushrooms (about 1 ounce)
- 3 cups hot water, more if needed
- 3½ cups canned low-sodium chicken broth or homemade stock, more if needed
- 3 tablespoons olive oil
- 1 onion, chopped
- 5 cloves garlic, minced
- 2 cups arborio rice
- 1¼ teaspoons salt
- 2 tablespoons butter
- ¼ teaspoon fresh-ground black pepper
- 2 ounces mild goat cheese, such as Montrachet, crumbled

  Grated Parmesan, for serving

1. Put the dried mushrooms in a medium bowl and pour the hot water over them. Soak until softened, about 20 minutes. Remove the mushrooms, reserving the soaking liquid, and chop them. Strain the liquid through a paper-towel-lined sieve into a medium saucepan. Add the broth to the pan and bring to a simmer.

2. In a medium pot, heat the oil over moderately low heat. Add the onion and garlic and cook, stirring occasionally, until the onion is translucent, about 5 minutes. Add the chopped mushrooms, the rice, and the salt and stir until the rice begins to turn opaque, about 2 minutes.

3. Add about ½ cup of the simmering broth to the rice and cook, stirring frequently, until the broth has been completely absorbed. The rice and broth should bubble gently; adjust the heat as needed. Continue cooking the rice, adding broth ½ cup at a time and allowing the rice to absorb it before adding the next ½ cup. Cook the rice in this way until tender, 25 to 30 minutes in all. The broth that hasn't been absorbed should be thickened by the starch from the rice. You may not need to use all of the liquid, or you may need more broth or some water.

4. Stir in the butter, pepper, and goat cheese. Serve the risotto with grated Parmesan.

CLAM RISOTTO WITH BACON AND CHIVES

If you buy just-shucked whole clams rather than already chopped clams in a container, use their liquid instead of the bottled clam juice; just be sure to strain it first through a paper towel to remove any grit.

WINE RECOMMENDATION
To make this risotto sing, serve it with a nicely acidic, herbal Verdicchio di Matelica or Verdicchio di Castelli dei Jesi.

SERVES 4

- 3 cups bottled clam juice
- 3 cups water, more if needed
- ¼ pound bacon, slices cut crosswise into thin strips
- 4 tablespoons olive oil
- 1 onion, chopped
- 3 cloves garlic, minced
- 2 cups arborio rice
- 1 cup dry white wine
- ¼ teaspoon salt, more if needed
- 3 tablespoons chopped fresh chives or scallion tops
- ¼ teaspoon fresh-ground black pepper
- 1 cup drained chopped clams

1. In a medium saucepan, bring the clam juice and water to a simmer.

2. In a large pot, cook the bacon until crisp. Remove the bacon from the pot and pour off all the fat. In the same pot, heat the oil over moderately low heat. Add the onion and garlic and cook, stirring occasionally, until the onion is translucent, about 5 minutes.

3. Add the rice to the pot and stir until it begins to turn opaque, about 2 minutes. Add the wine and salt and cook, stirring frequently, until all the wine has been absorbed.

4. Add the bacon and about ½ cup of the simmering clam juice to the rice and cook, stirring frequently, until the liquid has been completely absorbed. The rice and liquid should bubble gently; adjust the heat as needed. Continue cooking the rice, adding clam juice ½ cup at a time and allowing the rice to absorb the liquid before adding the next ½ cup. Cook the rice in this way until tender, 25 to 30 minutes in all. The liquid that hasn't been absorbed should be thickened by the starch from the rice. You may not need to use all of the clam juice, or you may need to add some water.

5. Stir in the chives, pepper, and clams. Cook, stirring, until the clams are just done, about 1 minute. Taste for salt and add more salt if needed.

RICE SALAD WITH CHICKEN AND ASPARAGUS

The rice soaks up the dressing as the salad sits, so if you make it more than half an hour ahead, it may dry out. In that case, just add some extra oil and lemon juice.

WINE RECOMMENDATION
Vinegar and asparagus are hard to match with wine, but sauvignon blanc can handle both. Look for one from Friuli, Alto Adige, or Collio.

SERVES 4

1/3 cup pine nuts

5 tablespoons wine vinegar

1 clove garlic, minced

1 tablespoon lemon juice

1 tablespoon Dijon mustard

2 teaspoons salt

3/4 teaspoon fresh-ground black pepper

9 tablespoons olive oil

2 cups rice, preferably arborio

1 pound asparagus, tough ends snapped off and discarded, stems cut into 1/4-inch pieces, tips left whole

1 1/3 pounds boneless chicken thighs (about 6)

1 large tomato, cut into 1/2-inch dice

1/2 cup chopped red onion

1. In a small frying pan, toast the pine nuts over moderately low heat, stirring frequently, until they are golden brown, about 5 minutes. Or toast in a 350° oven for 5 to 10 minutes.

2. In a small glass or stainless-steel bowl, using a fork, stir together the vinegar, garlic, lemon juice, mustard, 1 1/4 teaspoons of the salt, and 1/2 teaspoon of the pepper. Stir in the oil.

3. In a large pot of boiling, salted water, cook the rice until almost tender, about 10 minutes. Add the asparagus and cook until it and the rice are both done, about 5 minutes longer. Drain, rinse with cold water, and drain again. Transfer to a large glass or stainless-steel bowl.

4. Meanwhile, in a large frying pan, bring 1/4 inch of water to a simmer over moderately high heat. Sprinkle the chicken with the remaining 3/4 teaspoon salt and 1/4 teaspoon pepper and add to the pan. Cover, reduce the heat, and simmer, turning once, until cooked through, about 8 minutes. Remove the chicken, let cool slightly, and then cut into 1/2-inch chunks. Add to the rice and asparagus.

5. Add the tomato and red onion to the rice and then toss the salad with the dressing. Stir in the pine nuts just before serving.

POLENTA WITH EGGPLANT, ONION, AND TOMATOES

Sauté onion, eggplant, and tomatoes with plenty of garlic for a combination reminiscent of ratatouille. Then spoon this tasty vegetable stew over steaming Parmesan polenta to make a satisfying meal.

WINE RECOMMENDATION

A hearty dish needs a hearty wine. Open an earthy Salice Salentino from Dr. Cosimo Taurino. Made from the obscure negro amaro grape, it is one of the best wines from Italy's Apulia region.

SERVES 4

- 10 tablespoons olive oil
- 1 onion, chopped
- 5 cloves garlic, minced
- 1 large eggplant (about 1¾ pounds), cut into ½-inch cubes
- 2 tomatoes (about ¾ pound), cut into ½-inch pieces
- 1 cup canned crushed tomatoes in thick puree
- 3 tablespoons chopped fresh parsley
- 2¼ teaspoons salt
- ¼ teaspoon fresh-ground black pepper
- 4½ cups water
- 1⅓ cups coarse or medium cornmeal
- 6 tablespoons grated Parmesan

1. In a large nonstick frying pan, heat 1 tablespoon of the oil over moderate heat. Add the onion and garlic and cook, stirring occasionally, until the onion starts to brown, about 5 minutes. Remove. Heat 6 tablespoons of the oil in the same pan over moderately high heat. Add the eggplant and cook, stirring occasionally, until golden, about 10 minutes. Add the onion mixture, fresh and canned tomatoes, parsley, and 1 teaspoon of the salt. Simmer until thick, about 10 minutes. Stir in the pepper.

2. Meanwhile, in a medium saucepan, bring the water and the remaining 1¼ teaspoons of salt to a boil. Add the cornmeal in a slow stream, whisking constantly. Whisk in the remaining 3 tablespoons of oil. Reduce the heat and simmer, stirring frequently with a wooden spoon, until the polenta is thick, about 20 minutes. Stir in the Parmesan. Serve the hot polenta topped with the vegetables.

Polenta with Three Scoops of Cheese and Sautéed Shiitakes

Here's a heavenly concoction—warm, soft polenta covering scoops of creamy cheese, melting them with its heat. Chewy shiitake mushrooms, sautéed with garlic until golden brown, top the polenta. The combination of flavors and textures is divine.

WINE RECOMMENDATION

The tannins in a red wine will be tamed by the richness of the cheese in this dish, pushing the wine's flavor to the fore. A Rosso di Montalcino, Brunello's fruitier cousin, will demonstrate this delectably.

SERVES 4

4½ cups water, more if needed

Salt

1⅓ cups coarse or medium cornmeal

5 tablespoons olive oil

3 tablespoons grated Parmesan

1 cup whole-milk ricotta

1 cup mascarpone cheese

1 tablespoon butter

1 pound shiitake mushrooms, stems removed, caps cut into ¾-inch slices

2 cloves garlic, minced

3 tablespoons chopped fresh parsley

⅛ teaspoon fresh-ground black pepper

1. In a medium saucepan, bring the water and 1 teaspoon salt to a boil. Add the cornmeal in a slow stream, whisking constantly. Whisk in 3 tablespoons of the oil. Reduce the heat and simmer, stirring frequently with a wooden spoon, until the polenta is thick, about 20 minutes. Stir in the Parmesan. Remove from the heat but cover to keep warm.

2. Meanwhile, in a medium bowl, mix together the ricotta, mascarpone, and ⅛ teaspoon salt. Put in the refrigerator.

3. In a large frying pan, heat the remaining 2 tablespoons oil with the butter over moderately high heat. Add the mushrooms, garlic, and ¼ teaspoon salt. Cook, stirring, until the mushrooms are golden, 5 to 10 minutes. Stir in the parsley and pepper.

4. Stir the polenta. It should be thick but still pourable. If it's too thick, stir in more water. You may need as much as a cup. Using a large spoon or a medium ice-cream scoop, put three mounds of the cheese mixture onto each of four plates. Ladle the hot polenta over the mounds of cheese and top with the mushrooms.

POLENTA WITH MEAT SAUCE

This is comfort food at its finest: a quick-cooking Bolognese sauce, made with sausage, tomatoes, aromatic vegetables, and a touch of light cream, served over a mound of earthy polenta. Of course, you could put the same sauce over fettuccine instead.

WINE RECOMMENDATION
Homey food calls for a simple but flavorful red wine. For a touch of regional authenticity, select a Sangiovese di Romagna.

SERVES 4

- 4 tablespoons olive oil
- 1½ pounds mild Italian sausage, casings removed
- 2 carrots, chopped
- 1 onion, chopped
- 4 cloves garlic, minced
- ⅓ cup dry white wine
- 1½ cups canned crushed tomatoes in thick puree (from one 15-ounce can)
- ¾ cup canned low-sodium chicken broth or homemade stock
- 6 tablespoons chopped fresh parsley
- 1 bay leaf
- 1¾ teaspoons salt
- ¼ teaspoon fresh-ground black pepper
- 3 tablespoons light cream
- 4½ cups water
- 1⅓ cups coarse or medium cornmeal
- 3 tablespoons grated Parmesan, plus more for serving

1. In a large deep frying pan, heat 1 tablespoon of the oil over moderately high heat. Add the sausage and cook, breaking up the meat with a fork until no longer pink, about 3 minutes. Tilt the pan and spoon off all but 2 tablespoons fat. Reduce the heat to moderate. Add the carrots, onion, and garlic and cook, stirring occasionally, until the vegetables start to soften, about 5 minutes.

2. Stir in the wine and let simmer 3 minutes. Add the tomatoes, broth, 4 tablespoons of the parsley, the bay leaf, and ½ teaspoon of the salt. Simmer, covered, for 15 minutes. Uncover, add the pepper, and simmer 5 minutes longer. Remove the bay leaf. Stir in the cream and the remaining 2 tablespoons parsley.

3. Meanwhile, in a medium saucepan, bring the water and the remaining 1¼ teaspoons salt to a boil. Add the cornmeal in a slow stream, whisking constantly. Whisk in the remaining 3 tablespoons oil. Reduce the heat and simmer, stirring frequently with a wooden spoon, until the polenta is thick, about 20 minutes. Stir in the Parmesan.

4. Serve the polenta topped with the meat sauce. Pass additional Parmesan.

CHAPTER FIVE

Stovetop Cooking

CAULIFLOWER, BACON, AND PARMESAN FRITTATA

Eggs make perfect weeknight dinners; they cook quickly and taste great with an endless variety of ingredients. Here, bacon, sautéed cauliflower, and grated Parmesan complement each other in an original and satisfying frittata.

WINE RECOMMENDATION
Cheese and eggs both work well with red wine; their richness blunts the wine's tannin, while accentuating its fruitiness. A simple Chianti or Chianti Classico will be delightful.

SERVES 4

¼ pound bacon, slices cut crosswise into ¼-inch strips

8 large eggs

⅓ cup light cream

1 cup grated Parmesan

3 tablespoons chopped fresh parsley

⅛ teaspoon fresh-ground black pepper

2 tablespoons olive oil

1 tablespoon butter

1 small head cauliflower (about 1¼ pounds), cut into small florets

¼ teaspoon salt

4 cloves garlic, minced

1. In a 10-inch nonstick frying pan, cook the bacon until crisp. Remove. Pour off all the fat. In a large bowl, beat the eggs with the cream, Parmesan, parsley, and pepper until smooth. Add the cooled bacon.

2. In the same frying pan, heat the oil with the butter over moderately high heat. Add the cauliflower and salt and cook, stirring occasionally, until the cauliflower is golden and almost done, 10 to 15 minutes. Add the garlic and cook, stirring, 1 minute longer. Pour in the egg mixture and reduce the heat to low. Cook, covered, until the bottom of the frittata is golden brown and the top is almost set, 10 to 15 minutes.

3. Heat the broiler. Broil the frittata 6 inches from the heat, if possible, until the eggs are set and beginning to brown, about 3 minutes.

4. Lift up the edge of the frittata with a spatula and slide the frittata onto a plate. Cut it into wedges.

> ### TEST-KITCHEN TIP
>
> If the handle of your frying pan isn't ovenproof you can make it so. Protect it from the heat of the broiler by wrapping it with four layers of aluminum foil.

GARLIC SHRIMP IN TOMATO SAUCE

Chunky with capers and olives, this quick tomato sauce tastes much like the familiar *puttanesca* sauce that is usually served on pasta. We use it to coat shrimp sautéed with garlic and hot pepper.

WINE RECOMMENDATION
A smooth, medium-bodied red from southern Italy, such as a Cirò or Regaleali Rosso, will stand up to the gutsy sauce without overpowering the shrimp.

SERVES 4

- 3 tablespoons olive oil
- 2 pounds large shrimp, shelled
- 4 cloves garlic, minced
- 1 large pinch dried red-pepper flakes
- 1/4 teaspoon salt
- 1/4 teaspoon fresh-ground black pepper
- 2 medium tomatoes (about 3/4 pound), peeled and chopped
- 1 cup canned crushed tomatoes in thick puree
- 1 teaspoon chopped fresh rosemary, or 1/4 teaspoon dried rosemary
- 2 tablespoons drained capers
- 1/3 cup halved and pitted black olives

1. In a large nonstick frying pan, heat the oil over moderate heat. Add the shrimp, garlic, red-pepper flakes, salt, and black pepper and cook, stirring occasionally, until the shrimp are just done, about 5 minutes. Remove the shrimp with a slotted spoon.

2. Add the fresh tomatoes, canned tomatoes, rosemary, capers, and olives to the pan. Reduce the heat and simmer, covered, for 15 minutes. Stir in the shrimp and simmer until just heated through, about 1 minute.

VARIATION

Substitute four boneless, skinless **chicken breasts** for the shrimp. Make the sauce separately by sautéing the garlic for a minute, adding the red-pepper flakes, salt, and black pepper, and then proceeding with Step 2. In a medium frying pan, heat just one tablespoon of oil over moderate heat. Season the chicken breasts with a quarter teaspoon salt and an eighth teaspoon pepper and put them in the pan. Cook the chicken until brown, about five minutes. Turn and cook until almost done, about three minutes longer. Cover the pan, remove from the heat, and let steam five minutes. Top the chicken with the sauce.

101

STEAMED MUSSELS WITH TOMATO-AND-GARLIC BROTH

Mussels have three things going for them: They're cheap, quick to cook, and delicious. Using clean farmed mussels negates their one big drawback—the tedious chore of scrubbing and debearding.

WINE RECOMMENDATION
Every Mediterranean country has its version of shellfish in a tomato-based broth, and the wine of choice for each is an earthy, full-bodied pink wine. Here, seek out a Lacryma Christi rosé.

SERVES 4

- ¼ cup olive oil
- 1 onion, chopped fine
- 6 cloves garlic, minced
- 3 tablespoons chopped fresh parsley
- 2 cups drained canned tomatoes in thick puree, chopped (from one 28-ounce can)
- ¼ teaspoon dried thyme
- ¼ teaspoon dried red-pepper flakes
- 4 pounds mussels, scrubbed and debearded
- ⅛ teaspoon fresh-ground black pepper
  Salt, if needed
  Garlic toast (optional)

1. In a large pot, heat the oil over moderately low heat. Add the onion and garlic and cook, stirring occasionally, until the onion is translucent, about 5 minutes. Stir in the parsley, tomatoes, thyme, and red-pepper flakes. Reduce the heat and simmer, partially covered, for 25 minutes, stirring occasionally.

2. Discard any mussels that have broken shells or that don't clamp shut when tapped. Add the mussels to the pot. Cover; bring to a boil. Cook, shaking the pot occasionally, just until the mussels open, about 3 minutes. Remove the open mussels. Continue to boil, uncovering the pot as necessary to remove the mussels as soon as their shells open. Discard any that do not open.

3. Stir the black pepper into the broth. Taste the broth and, if needed, add salt. Ladle the broth over the mussels and serve with the garlic toast.

GARLIC TOAST

- 4 ½-inch slices country bread
- 1 clove garlic, halved

Heat the broiler. Put the bread on a baking sheet and broil, turning once, until crisp and brown on the outside but still slightly soft in the center, about 3 minutes. Rub one side of each slice with the cut-side of the garlic.

SAUTÉED WHOLE TROUT WITH SAGE AND WHITE WINE

The garnish of fried sage leaves makes a delectable crisp treat, but of course the trout is still good without it. You can usually sauté four small trout at the same time in a large frying pan, but if they're crowded, cook the fish in two pans or two batches.

WINE RECOMMENDATION

Farm-raised trout are mild, so a pinot grigio or pinot bianco from northeastern Italy will make a superb accompaniment. A gamier wild fish can use a stronger wine such as a chardonnay.

SERVES 4

4   trout (about ¾ pound each), cleaned

3   tablespoons olive oil

5   tablespoons cold butter

    Salt

    Fresh-ground black pepper

    About 36 fresh sage leaves or 1 teaspoon dried sage

⅓   cup dry white wine

1. Rinse the fish and dry the surface and the cavity of each thoroughly with paper towels. In a large nonstick frying pan, heat 2 tablespoons of the oil with 1 tablespoon of the butter over moderately high heat. Sprinkle the trout with ½ teaspoon salt and ¼ teaspoon pepper. Put the trout in the pan and cook until golden, about 5 minutes. Turn and cook until golden on the second side and just done, 5 to 10 minutes longer. Remove; wipe out the pan.

2. In the same pan, heat the remaining 1 tablespoon oil over moderately high heat. Add the sage leaves and cook until crisp, about 1 minute. Alternatively, add the dried sage and cook, stirring, for 1 minute. Pour the oil and sage over the fish. Wipe out the pan.

3. Add the wine to the pan. Boil until reduced to approximately 3 tablespoons, 1 to 2 minutes. Reduce the heat to the lowest setting and whisk in the remaining 4 tablespoons butter, ⅛ teaspoon salt, and ⅛ teaspoon pepper. Whisk in any accumulated juices and oil from the trout. Pour the sauce around the fish and serve.

TEST-KITCHEN TIP

For a creamy emulsified butter sauce, don't just put the butter in the pan and let it melt; instead, stick a whisk in the cold butter and stir it around the bottom of the pan over the lowest possible heat. This way, the butter just softens into a sauce instead of melting into a puddle.

SAUTÉED CHICKEN BREASTS WITH SALSA VERDE

Perk up boneless chicken breasts with piquant salsa verde. In Italy this tangy green sauce often accompanies poached chicken or fish and boiled meat. We think it's delicious on sautéed and grilled foods as well.

WINE RECOMMENDATION

Clean, crisp, lightly fruity Italian whites were made for dishes like this. A Soave Classico or Vernaccia di San Gimignano will stand back and let the main course take center stage.

SERVES 4

- 2/3 cup lightly packed flat-leaf parsley leaves
- 3 tablespoons drained capers
- 3 cloves garlic, 1 whole, 2 minced
- 4 teaspoons lemon juice
- 1 teaspoon anchovy paste
- 1/2 teaspoon Dijon mustard
- 3/4 teaspoon salt
- 1/4 teaspoon fresh-ground black pepper
- 1/2 cup plus 1 tablespoon olive oil
- 4 boneless, skinless chicken breasts (about 1 1/3 pounds in all)
- 1/4 teaspoon dried thyme

1. Put the parsley, capers, the whole garlic clove, the lemon juice, anchovy paste, mustard, 1/2 teaspoon of the salt, and 1/8 teaspoon of the pepper into a food processor or blender. Pulse just to chop, six to eight times. With the machine running, add the 1/2 cup oil in a thin stream to make a slightly coarse puree. Leave this salsa verde in the food processor; if necessary, pulse to re-emulsify just before serving.

2. In a large frying pan, heat the remaining tablespoon of oil over moderate heat. Season the chicken breasts with the remaining 1/4 teaspoon salt and 1/8 teaspoon pepper and the thyme and put them in the hot pan. Cook the chicken until brown, about 5 minutes. Turn and cook until almost done, about 3 minutes longer. Add the minced garlic and cook for 30 seconds, stirring. Cover the pan, remove from the heat, and let steam 5 minutes. Serve the breasts with their juices and then the salsa verde poured over the top.

BRAISED CHICKEN THIGHS WITH OLIVES AND BASIL

Though it only cooks for half an hour, this dish has the satisfying, melded flavor of a long-simmered stew. Part of the explanation is that the garlic cloves are cooked whole and them mashed into the sauce. You'll always get a more mellow flavor from whole cloves than from chopped or crushed garlic.

WINE RECOMMENDATION

Italy has three great red grapes. Nebbiolo and sangiovese are well known, but the robust aglianico grape deserves at least the same regard. This dish is a great opportunity to sample either of its best wines, Taurasi or Aglianico del Vulture.

SERVES 4

- 1 tablespoon olive oil
- 8 chicken thighs (about 3 pounds in all)
- 1 teaspoon salt
  Fresh-ground black pepper
- 1 onion, chopped
- 12 cloves garlic, peeled
- 2 teaspoons chopped fresh rosemary, or
  3/4 teaspoon dried rosemary
- 1/2 cup dry white wine
- 1/2 cup canned low-sodium chicken broth or homemade stock
- 1 cup canned crushed tomatoes in thick puree
- 1/3 cup halved and pitted black olives
- 1/3 cup chopped fresh basil

1. In a large deep frying pan, heat the oil over moderately high heat. Season the chicken with 1/2 teaspoon of the salt and 1/4 teaspoon pepper. Put the chicken in the pan and brown well on both sides, about 8 minutes in all. Remove. Pour off all but 1 tablespoon of the fat. Reduce the heat to moderately low.

2. Add the onion and garlic and cook, stirring occasionally, until the onion starts to soften, about 5 minutes. Add the rosemary and wine. Bring to a simmer, scraping the bottom of the pan to dislodge any brown bits. Boil until the wine is reduced to approximately 1/4 cup, 1 to 2 minutes.

3. Add the broth, tomatoes, olives, the remaining 1/2 teaspoon salt, and the chicken, skin-side up, with any accumulated juices. Cover and simmer until the chicken is just done, 20 to 25 minutes. Push the chicken to the side of the pan and then mash the garlic cloves with a fork. Stir in 1/8 teaspoon pepper and the basil, bring just to a simmer, and serve.

VEAL CHOPS MILANESE WITH SAGE

To get half-inch veal chops, the butcher will have to cut two chops per rib rather than just cutting between ribs. Half of the chops will have a rib bone and half won't. Ask the butcher to pound the chops for you to an eighth of an inch thick, or do the flattening at home with a meat pounder or the bottom of a heavy frying pan.

WINE RECOMMENDATION
Try a Sankt Magdalener riesling or, if you can't find one, a German kabinett halbtrocken riesling. You'll be happily surprised by how good the combination of the wine and the veal chops will taste.

SERVES 4

1 egg
¼ teaspoon salt
⅛ teaspoon fresh-ground black pepper
¾ cup fine dry bread crumbs
1 tablespoon chopped fresh sage, or 1 teaspoon dried sage
4 ½-inch-thick veal rib chops (about 5 ounces each), chine bone removed, chops pounded to ⅛ inch thick
5 tablespoons butter
1 lemon, cut into wedges

1. Beat the egg to mix with the salt and the pepper. Combine the bread crumbs and the fresh or dried sage. Dip the veal chops (including the rib bone if the chop has one) into the beaten egg and then into the bread crumbs. Shake off the excess bread crumbs.

2. In a large nonstick frying pan, melt the butter over moderately low heat. Put the coated veal chops in the pan and cook until golden, about 4 minutes. Turn and cook until golden and just done, about 3 minutes longer. Serve with the lemon wedges.

VARIATIONS

■ These chops are also excellent, and in fact more traditional, **without** the **sage**.
■ You can throw tradition to the winds and sauté the chops **without pounding**. They'll need another minute of cooking per side.
■ Another possibility is to make this with **pork chops**, either pounded or not.

TEST-KITCHEN TIP

To ensure a crisp coating, keep the heat steady at moderately low. Don't be tempted to turn it down or the crumbs won't brown to a crunchy gold.

PORK CHOPS WITH MARSALA AND FENNEL

Thin slices of fennel, a shot of dry marsala, and a touch of tomato paste combine to make a quick, intense pan sauce for sautéed pork chops. If you prefer, substitute red wine for the marsala.

WINE RECOMMENDATION

A well-made Nebbiolo delle Langhe has earthy and herbal flavors to blend nicely with fennel and just the right amount of tannin and dried-cherry fruitiness for the marsala and pork.

SERVES 4

- 1 tablespoon olive oil, more if needed
- 4 pork chops, about ¾ inch thick (about 2½ pounds in all)
  Salt
  Fresh-ground black pepper
- 1 onion, chopped
- 1 fennel bulb, cut into thin slices
- 4 cloves garlic, minced
- ½ cup dry marsala
- ⅔ cup canned low-sodium chicken broth or homemade stock
- 1 tablespoon tomato paste
- 3 tablespoons chopped fresh parsley

1. In a large frying pan, heat the oil over moderate heat. Season the pork chops with ¼ teaspoon each salt and pepper. Put the chops in the pan. Cook, turning once, until browned and done to medium, about 5 minutes per side. Remove and put in a warm place.

2. If necessary, add oil to the pan to make about 2 tablespoons fat. Add the onion, fennel, and ⅛ teaspoon salt. Cook, covered, stirring occasionally, until soft, about 10 minutes. Uncover and add the garlic. Cook, stirring, 1 minute longer. Add the marsala. Bring to a boil, scraping the bottom of the pan to dislodge any brown bits. Boil until reduced to approximately ¼ cup, 1 to 2 minutes.

3. Stir in the broth, tomato paste, 2 tablespoons of the parsley, ½ teaspoon salt, and any accumulated juices from the meat. Bring to a simmer and cook, covered, until the sauce thickens and the fennel is tender, about 5 minutes. Add the remaining tablespoon parsley, ⅛ teaspoon pepper, and the pork chops. Cook until just heated through, 2 to 3 minutes.

VARIATION

Instead of chops, sauté one-inch-thick medallions of **pork tenderloin**, seasoned with salt and pepper, until just done, about two minutes per side.

BRAISED PORK WITH BACON AND ONIONS

Certain dishes of northeast Italy, such as this one, are influenced by the region's proximity to Austria and Germany. The somewhat acidic flavor of the pork is similar to that of German sauerbraten, but the garlic and rosemary add a distinctly Italian touch.

WINE RECOMMENDATION

In Austria, Germany, or Alsace, the classic accompaniment for this type of dish is gewürztraminer. Look for one of the superb examples from the Alto Adige or Germany's Pfalz region and you'll understand why.

SERVES 4

- 2 slices bacon cut crosswise into ½-inch strips
- 2 pork tenderloins (about 1¾ pounds in all)
  Salt
- ½ teaspoon fresh-ground black pepper
- 1 tablespoon olive oil
- 2 onions, sliced thin
- 2 cloves garlic, minced
- ½ cup dry white wine
- 1 cup canned low-sodium chicken broth or homemade stock
- 1 teaspoon wine vinegar
- 3 cloves
- 2 bay leaves
- 1 sprig rosemary, or ½ teaspoon dried rosemary, crumbled

1. In a large deep stainless-steel frying pan or a Dutch oven, cook the bacon over moderate heat until crisp. Remove with a slotted spoon. Season the pork with ½ teaspoon salt and ¼ teaspoon of the pepper. Increase the heat to moderately high. Put the pork in the pan and brown on all sides, turning, about 8 minutes in all. Remove.

2. Reduce the heat to moderate and add the oil to the pan. Add the onions and garlic and cook, stirring occasionally, until the onions are golden, about 5 minutes. Add the wine and simmer for 3 minutes.

3. Stir in the broth, vinegar, cloves, bay leaves, rosemary, ¼ teaspoon salt, and the pork with any accumulated juices. Bring to a simmer. Cover and simmer, turning the meat once, until the pork is just done, about 10 minutes. Remove the meat from the pan, transfer to a carving board, and leave to rest in a warm spot for 5 minutes. Stir the remaining ¼ teaspoon pepper and ⅛ teaspoon salt into the pan and simmer until the sauce thickens slightly, about 3 minutes. Remove the bay leaves, rosemary sprig, and cloves. Cut the meat into thin slices and serve topped with the sauce.

SAUSAGES, POTATOES, AND ARTICHOKE HEARTS IN TOMATO BROTH

Simmering chunks of potato, Italian sausages, and artichoke hearts in a tomatoey broth melds their flavors into a savory stew. Sop up the plentiful broth with crusty bread.

WINE RECOMMENDATION
This dish suggests cabernet sauvignon or sangiovese as a wine partner. You can have both in Carmignano, a rich Tuscan red based on the two grapes. Many good Chianti Classicos also have a high percentage of cabernet sauvignon and will work well here.

SERVES 4

1	tablespoon olive oil
1½	pounds mild Italian sausages
3	cloves garlic, cut into thin slices
1½	pounds boiling potatoes (about 5), cut into 1-inch chunks
½	teaspoon dried thyme
⅓	cup dry white wine
1¼	cups canned low-sodium chicken broth or homemade stock
1	cup canned crushed tomatoes in thick puree
1½	cups drained and rinsed halved canned artichoke hearts (one 14-ounce can)
6	tablespoons chopped fresh parsley
½	teaspoon salt
½	teaspoon fresh-ground black pepper

1. In a large stainless-steel pot, heat the oil over moderately high heat. Add the sausages and brown well, about 10 minutes. Remove. Pour off all but 1 tablespoon of the fat.

2. Reduce the heat to moderate. Add the garlic, potatoes, and thyme. Cook, stirring occasionally, until the potatoes are lightly browned, about 5 minutes. Add the wine and boil until reduced to approximately 3 tablespoons, 2 to 3 minutes.

3. Stir in the broth, tomatoes, artichoke hearts, 4 tablespoons of the parsley, the salt, and the sausages. Bring to a simmer and cook, partially covered, until the potatoes are tender, about 30 minutes. Add the remaining 2 tablespoons parsley and the pepper.

VARIATIONS

Substitute:
- **Rosemary** for the thyme
- **Red wine** for the white wine
- **Hot Italian sausage** for the mild

SAUTÉED STEAKS WITH RED WINE AND PEPPERS

Chuck steaks have a full beefy flavor and stay remarkably tender when cooked to a rosy medium rare. If you like steaks well done, though, choose a different cut or the meat will be chewy. The red wine is meant to flavor the onion and peppers, not to make a sauce. Boil it until it's completely absorbed by the vegetables.

WINE RECOMMENDATION
With these steaks, you need a richly flavored, full-bodied red. Take a break from the same old cabernet sauvignon and try a refosco, a robust yet surprisingly sophisticated wine from the extreme northeast corner of Italy.

SERVES 4

    4   tablespoons olive oil
    1   large onion, sliced thin
 1½   teaspoons dried oregano
    1   large clove garlic, minced
    1   red bell pepper, sliced thin
    1   green bell pepper, sliced thin
    4   top chuck steaks (about 2 pounds in all),
        pounded to ½-inch thick
    1   teaspoon salt
  ¾   teaspoon fresh-ground black pepper
  ¾   cup red wine

1. Heat 2 tablespoons of the oil in a medium frying pan over moderately low heat. Stir in the onion, oregano, garlic, and bell peppers. Cook, covered, until the vegetables are soft, about 5 minutes.

2. In a large stainless-steel frying pan, heat the remaining 2 tablespoons of the oil over moderately high heat. Season the steaks with ½ teaspoon salt and ¼ teaspoon black pepper. Put the steaks in the hot pan and cook until browned, 3 to 4 minutes. Turn and cook until done to medium rare, 3 to 4 minutes longer. Remove.

3. Add the bell-pepper mixture, the wine, and the remaining ½ teaspoon each salt and black pepper to the large frying pan. Boil until the wine is completely absorbed, about 5 minutes. Serve the steak topped with the vegetables.

POUNDING MEAT

Pounding tenderizes meat and also makes it thinner so it will cook more quickly. Cover the meat with a piece of plastic wrap or waxed paper and then flatten the steak with a traditional meat pounder or the bottom of a heavy frying pan. Or, ask your butcher to pound the meat for you.

LIVER AND ONIONS VENETIAN STYLE

Those who like liver and onions will love this—as will many who don't. With sweet caramelized onions; melting, perfectly cooked liver; and a sprinkling of sage, this earthy dish makes us swoon with pleasure. Serve it over creamy polenta (see Step 2, page 91).

WINE RECOMMENDATION
Brunello di Montalcino is Tuscany's most exalted wine because it offers a combination of richness, power, and elegance unmatched by any other in the region. Serve one here for a sumptuous experience. A more affordable option is Rosso di Montalcino, a sort of scaled-down brunello.

SERVES 4

    4   tablespoons olive oil

    2   tablespoons butter

    4   onions, sliced thin

    ¾   teaspoon salt

    1½ pounds ½-inch-thick slices calf's liver, cut into 1½-inch squares

    ¼   teaspoon fresh-ground black pepper

    6   fresh sage leaves, or ½ teaspoon dried sage

1. In a large nonstick frying pan, heat 3 tablespoons of the oil with 1½ tablespoons of the butter over moderately high heat. Add the onions and cook, stirring occasionally, for 10 minutes. Stir in ¼ teaspoon of the salt. Reduce the heat to moderate and cook, stirring frequently, until the onions are well browned, about 5 minutes longer. Remove.

2. Sprinkle the liver with the remaining ½ teaspoon salt and the pepper. In the same pan, heat the remaining tablespoon oil and ½ tablespoon butter over high heat. When the pan is very hot, add the liver and sage. Cook, stirring, until just done, 1 to 2 minutes. Remove from the heat, return the onions to the pan, and toss.

HOW TO COOK LIVER

Forget all the bitter, grainy liver you may have had. The way to make liver taste good is primarily a matter of resisting the temptation to overcook it. It should be seared to keep the juices from escaping and should be slightly pink inside, not dingy gray. Use high heat bravely and briefly.

CHAPTER SIX

From the Grill or Broiler

SHRIMP WITH CANNELLINI-BEAN SALAD

Shrimp and sage-scented white beans is a popular Italian combination. Use only high-quality canned beans—Goya is a reliable brand—or your salad will surely be mushy.

WINE RECOMMENDATION
The beans and the shrimp require a white with good body and full flavor. Tocai friulano gives you both, while at the same time contributing a lively acidity that refreshes the palate.

SERVES 4

1½   pounds large shrimp, shelled
½   cup olive oil
2   cloves garlic, minced
½   teaspoon salt
1   small onion, minced
1   tablespoon chopped flat-leaf parsley
1½   tablespoons chopped fresh sage leaves, or 1½ teaspoons dried sage
1   tablespoon wine vinegar
¼   teaspoon fresh-ground black pepper
3⅓   cups drained and rinsed canned cannellini beans (two 15-ounce cans)

1. Light the grill or heat the broiler. Thread the shrimp onto four skewers. In a shallow glass dish, combine ¼ cup of the oil with the garlic and ¼ teaspoon of the salt. Add the skewers and turn to coat the shrimp. Set aside.

2. In a medium bowl, combine the onion with the remaining ¼ cup oil and ¼ teaspoon salt, the parsley, sage, vinegar, and pepper. Gently stir in the beans.

3. Grill or broil the shrimp, turning once, until just done, about 5 minutes in all. Serve the shrimp with the bean salad.

TEST-KITCHEN TIP

We put the shrimp on skewers before grilling so that they don't fall through the grate. If you don't have metal skewers, the disposable wooden ones work just fine. Soak them in water for ten or fifteen minutes before using them so that they don't burn up. Or you could use a grilling basket.

GRILLED SQUID SALAD

Grill the squid whole and then cut them into slices for this salad. Not only is it easier (no squid rings falling through the grate), but small pieces risk cooking too quickly and becoming rubbery.

WINE RECOMMENDATION
A light, high-acid wine is a must to stand up to the lemon and vinegar in the dressing here. To highlight the squid, serve a vibrant, fruity pinot grigio from the Alto Adige.

SERVES 4

2   pounds cleaned squid

¾   cup olive oil

1   teaspoon salt

¼   cup lemon juice (from about 1 lemon)

2   teaspoons wine vinegar

¼   teaspoon fresh-ground black pepper

3   tablespoons thin-sliced basil leaves

½   head green leaf lettuce, torn into bite-size pieces (about 1 quart)

¼   cup drained sliced pimientos (2 ounces)

½   cup halved and pitted black olives

4   scallions including green tops, sliced thin

1. Light the grill. In a medium bowl, toss the squid with ¼ cup of the oil and ¾ teaspoon of the salt.

2. In a large glass or stainless-steel bowl, combine the lemon juice, vinegar, the remaining ¼ teaspoon salt, and the pepper. Stir in the remaining ½ cup oil with a fork. Stir in the basil.

3. Grill the squid quickly over high heat, turning once, until just done, 1 to 2 minutes per side. Remove. When cool enough to handle, cut the bodies into ½-inch rings and cut the tentacles in half. Add the squid, lettuce, pimientos, olives, and scallions to the dressing and toss.

VARIATION

Shrimp can replace the squid. Toss a pound and a half of large shelled shrimp with the oil and salt, as in Step 1, and grill or broil them until just done, turning once, about five minutes in all.

GRILLED WHOLE SNAPPER

Cover the grill while you're cooking the fish to keep the flesh moist and to prevent flare-ups that would burn the bread crumbs. We like to use a grill basket, which helps prevent sticking, but you can cook the fish directly on the grill. Just be sure it's impeccably clean, and turn the fish carefully so you don't lose the crust.

WINE RECOMMENDATION
Snapper is a delicate fish, and though grilling adds some stronger flavors, you'll be best off with a fairly neutral but crisp white. Orvieto Classico strikes the perfect balance.

SERVES 4

2   1¼- to 1½-pound whole red snappers, cleaned and scaled

1   teaspoon salt

2   large sprigs rosemary plus 1 tablespoon chopped fresh rosemary, or 2 teaspoons dried rosemary, crumbled

3   tablespoons olive oil

2   cloves garlic, minced

1   tablespoon dry bread crumbs
    Lemon wedges, for serving

1. Light the grill. Rinse the fish; dry the surfaces and cavities thoroughly. Cut shallow incisions in a crisscross pattern, about 1 inch apart, in each side of both fish. Season each fish cavity with ⅛ teaspoon of the salt. Put a rosemary sprig in each cavity or rub with ½ teaspoon dried rosemary. Rub the surface of both fish using 2 tablespoons of the oil, the garlic, the chopped fresh or remaining 1 teaspoon dried rosemary, and the remaining ¾ teaspoon salt. Sprinkle the bread crumbs on both sides of each fish. Drizzle both sides with the remaining tablespoon oil.

2. Put the fish in a grill basket or onto a very clean grill rack. Cook over moderately high heat for 7 minutes. Turn and grill until golden and just done, about 7 minutes longer. Remove the fish carefully so it doesn't stick.

3. Serve the fish on a platter. Run a knife between the flesh and the bones and lift off the fillet. Turn the fish over and repeat. Repeat with the other fish. Pass lemon wedges.

ROASTED WHOLE SNAPPER

Purchase one three-and-a-half-pound snapper instead of two smaller ones. Prepare the fish in the same manner through Step 1, using one-quarter teaspoon salt and both sprigs or one teaspoon rosemary in the cavity. Heat the oven to 450° instead of lighting the grill. Put the fish on a rack in a roasting pan; cook until just done, about twenty minutes. No need to turn the fish while cooking.

TUNA STEAKS WITH LEMON CAPER SAUCE

Grilled tuna steaks are one of life's simple pleasures, satisfying even when unadorned. Here they're made better yet with a quick lemon-and-caper sauce, whose pleasant tartness balances the richness of the fish.

WINE RECOMMENDATION
Though grilled tuna is superb with pinot noir, here the acidic sauce calls for a white wine. Gavi, Piedmont's cortese-based white, has just the right limelike accents to complement the tangy capers and lemon.

SERVES 4

3	tablespoons drained capers
1½	tablespoons lemon juice
¼	cup chopped fresh parsley
¾	teaspoon salt
½	teaspoon fresh-ground black pepper
8	tablespoons olive oil
4	tuna steaks, about ¾ inch thick (about 2 pounds in all)

1. Light the grill or heat the broiler. In a small glass or stainless-steel bowl, mash the capers with a fork. Stir in the lemon juice, parsley, ½ teaspoon of the salt, and ¼ teaspoon of the pepper and then 6 tablespoons of the oil.

2. Coat the tuna with the remaining 2 tablespoons oil. Sprinkle with the remaining ¼ teaspoon each salt and pepper. Grill or broil the tuna for 4 minutes. Turn and cook until done to your taste, 3 to 4 minutes longer for medium rare. Serve the tuna topped with the sauce.

VARIATIONS

The lemon-and-caper sauce tastes great on almost any grilled fish. **Swordfish** or **salmon** steaks are especially good choices. Just adjust the cooking time according to the thickness of the fish.

131

GRILLED CHICKEN BREASTS WITH LEMON AND THYME

A bold mixture of red-pepper flakes, garlic, thyme, lemon juice, and olive oil serves as a spicy marinade for bone-in chicken breasts. If you want your chicken spicier still, increase the red pepper or leave the breasts in the marinade for an hour or two.

WINE RECOMMENDATION

Red pepper can be difficult to pair with wine as it accentuates the bitterness of the alcohol. So, bypass high-alcohol wines and try an herbal, light-bodied sauvignon blanc from Collio.

SERVES 4

1½   tablespoons lemon juice

¼   teaspoon dried thyme

½   teaspoon dried red-pepper flakes

1   clove garlic, minced

¼   cup olive oil

¼   teaspoon salt

¼   teaspoon fresh-ground black pepper

4   bone-in chicken breasts (about 2¼ pounds in all)

1. Light the grill or heat the broiler. In a shallow dish, combine the lemon juice with the thyme, red-pepper flakes, garlic, oil, salt, and black pepper. Coat the chicken with the mixture.

2. Grill the chicken breasts over moderately high heat or broil them for 8 to 10 minutes. Turn and cook until the chicken is just done, about 10 minutes longer.

VARIATIONS

■ Try any dried herb you like in place of the thyme. **Marjoram**, **oregano**, **rosemary**, or **sage** are all good choices.

■ Use **boneless, skinless chicken breasts** instead of bone-in breasts. Grill them until just done, about five minutes per side over moderately high heat.

■ Use a **quartered chicken** instead of bone-in breasts. Cook the breast sections as directed in Step 2 and allow thirteen minutes per side for the leg quarters.

CHICKEN SALAD WITH GORGONZOLA, WALNUTS, AND FIGS

Mild grilled chicken, tender spinach leaves, bitter radicchio, sweet chewy figs, toasted walnuts, and creamy tangy Gorgonzola cheese—this combination of contrasting flavors and textures is unforgettable.

WINE RECOMMENDATION
Avoid big reds; walnuts have quite a bit of tannin, which when combined with tannic wines can create overwhelming dryness. A fresh, fruity Bardolino is perfect for this complex salad.

SERVES 4

2	cups water
6	dried figs
⅔	cup walnut halves
1⅓	pounds boneless, skinless chicken breasts (about 4)
1	tablespoon plus ⅓ cup olive oil
½	teaspoon salt
½	teaspoon fresh-ground black pepper
2	teaspoons chopped fresh rosemary, or ½ teaspoon dried rosemary, crumbled
1	head radicchio, torn into 1-inch pieces (about 1½ quarts)
12	ounces spinach, large stems removed and leaves washed (about 1½ quarts)
1½	tablespoons wine vinegar
¼	pound Gorgonzola, crumbled

1. Put the water and the figs in a small saucepan. Bring to a boil, turn off the heat, and let stand until the figs are plump, 10 to 15 minutes. Drain the figs and cut them in quarters.

2. In a small frying pan, toast the walnuts over moderately low heat, stirring frequently, until golden brown, about 5 minutes. Or toast them in a 350° oven for 5 to 10 minutes.

3. Light the grill or heat the broiler. Rub the chicken with the 1 tablespoon oil and sprinkle with ¼ teaspoon of the salt, ¼ teaspoon of the pepper, and the rosemary. Grill or broil the chicken until just done, about 5 minutes per side. When cool enough to handle, cut into ¼-inch slices.

4. Put the radicchio and the spinach in a large bowl. Add the remaining ⅓ cup oil and ¼ teaspoon each salt and pepper and toss. Add the vinegar and toss again. Put the radicchio and spinach on plates. Top with the sliced chicken, and then the Gorgonzola and walnuts. Put some of the figs in the center of each salad.

PEPPERED CORNISH HENS AND ASPARAGUS WITH LEMON AND MARJORAM

The same lemony marjoram-flavored marinade coats both the hens and the asparagus spears. Marjoram loses much of its taste during drying, so if you don't have fresh, you might prefer to use its brawnier cousin, oregano. In that case, use just three-quarters teaspoon of dried.

WINE RECOMMENDATION
Asparagus, which creates problems for most wines, is a natural with sauvignon blanc. Look for one of the many superb examples now being produced in Friuli and Collio.

SERVES 4

6 tablespoons olive oil

¼ cup lemon juice (from about 1 lemon)

¾ teaspoon salt

2 teaspoons fresh-ground black pepper

1 tablespoon fresh marjoram, or
1½ teaspoons dried marjoram

2 Cornish hens (about 1¼ pounds each), halved

1 pound asparagus

1. Light the grill. In a small glass or stainless-steel bowl, combine the oil with the lemon juice, salt, pepper, and marjoram. Put the hens in a glass dish or stainless-steel pan. Pour ¼ cup of the marinade over them and turn to coat.

2. Snap off and discard the tough ends of the asparagus spears, and then toss the trimmed asparagus spears with 2 tablespoons of the remaining marinade.

3. Cook the hens over moderate heat for 12 minutes, basting with the remaining marinade. Turn and cook, basting, until golden and just done, about 12 minutes longer. Grill the asparagus, turning once, until tender, about 12 minutes. Serve the hens with the asparagus alongside.

VARIATIONS

Instead of, or in addition to, the asparagus, grill some **bell peppers**, **mushrooms**, **eggplant**, **zucchini**, or **red onions**. If you run out of marinade, just toss the remaining vegetables with a little olive oil and salt before grilling and baste the hens with plain olive oil.

VEAL CHOPS WITH FRESH-TOMATO SAUCE

You'll want to use the best summer tomatoes you can find for this uncooked sauce. A touch of balsamic vinegar intensifies both the sweet and sour flavors of the tomatoes. Use a slotted spoon when serving the sauce so the watery liquid that drains off the tomatoes stays in the bowl.

WINE RECOMMENDATION

Don't bury the veal and its light sauce under a big, tannic wine. Dolcetto, with its fresh cherry and herb flavors and crisp, refreshing bite, is a much better choice.

SERVES 4

5½ tablespoons olive oil

¼ cup red wine

¾ teaspoon salt

Fresh-ground black pepper

2 cloves garlic, smashed

4 veal loin chops, about 1 inch thick (about 3 pounds in all)

1¼ pounds vine-ripened tomatoes (about 4), chopped

1½ tablespoons chopped mixed fresh herbs, such as parsley, basil, and chives

½ teaspoon balsamic vinegar

1. Light the grill or heat the broiler. In a shallow dish, combine 4 tablespoons of the oil with the wine, ½ teaspoon of the salt, ¼ teaspoon pepper, and the garlic. Add the veal chops and turn to coat.

2. In a medium glass or stainless-steel bowl, combine the tomatoes with the remaining ¼ teaspoon salt, the remaining 1½ tablespoons oil, the herbs, vinegar, and a large pinch of pepper.

3. Grill the chops over high heat or broil them for 4 to 5 minutes. Turn and cook until just done, 4 to 5 minutes longer. Serve the veal chops topped with the tomato sauce.

VARIATION

If you're in a rush or tomatoes are out of season, **skip the tomato sauce**. The chops are perfectly fine on their own.

LAMB CHOPS WITH GARLIC AND OLIVE OIL

Tender rib chops take only a few minutes per side to cook but are elegant enough to serve to company. Coat them with just the garlic and oil, or try one of our herb variations.

WINE RECOMMENDATION
Grilled lamb chops are the perfect foil for the rich cassis and herbal flavors of cabernet sauvignon. Your best bet here is a so-called super Tuscan. Though the most famous wines, such as Sassicaia and Tignanello, fetch astronomical prices, many excellent values can also be found.

SERVES 4

6 tablespoons olive oil

2 cloves garlic, minced

½ teaspoon salt

¼ teaspoon fresh-ground black pepper

8 lamb rib chops, about 1 inch thick (about 2¾ pounds in all)

1. Light the grill or heat the broiler. In a shallow dish, combine 4 tablespoons of the oil with the garlic, salt, and pepper. Add the lamb chops and turn to coat.

2. Grill over high heat or broil the lamb chops for 5 minutes, basting with the remaining 2 tablespoons oil. Turn and cook until done, about 5 minutes longer.

VARIATIONS

■ Add four teaspoons of chopped fresh **rosemary** to the garlic and oil mixture.
■ Add three tablespoons of chopped fresh **sage** and an additional tablespoon olive oil to the garlic and oil mixture.
■ Use lamb **loin chops** instead of rib chops.

TEST-KITCHEN TIPS

■ When grilling quick-cooking items such as chops, turn them only once. If you leave the meat alone for a few minutes, it will have a chance to form a nice brown crust. If you move it too soon, the meat will stick, and you'll pull off the incipient crust. Once that brown edge forms, the meat is easy to move.
■ When you do turn the meat, use tongs or a spatula. Never poke a fork into the meat or the precious juices will escape.

SARDINIAN LAMB KABOBS OVER COUSCOUS

Grill or broil skewers of lemon-and-thyme-scented lamb, and then serve them atop a garlicky Sardinian couscous full of cauliflower, currants, and pine nuts.

WINE RECOMMENDATION
Cabernet sauvignons from Friuli and Collio are often dismissed because they're light-bodied; however, their herbaceous flavors make them perfect for these kabobs.

SERVES 4

1/3 cup pine nuts

1½ pounds boneless leg of lamb, cut into 1½-inch cubes

8 tablespoons olive oil

2 teaspoons dried thyme

4 tablespoons lemon juice

1 onion, chopped

1 small head cauliflower (about 1¼ pounds), cut into small florets

4 cloves garlic, minced

2 teaspoons salt

¼ teaspoon saffron (optional)

¾ teaspoon fresh-ground black pepper

1 cup canned crushed tomatoes in thick puree

1¾ cups canned low-sodium chicken broth or homemade stock

½ cup currants

1½ cups couscous

¼ cup chopped fresh parsley

1. In a small frying pan, toast the pine nuts over moderately low heat, stirring frequently, until golden brown, about 5 minutes. Light the grill or heat the broiler. In a glass dish or stainless-steel pan, combine the lamb, 6 tablespoons of the oil, the thyme, and 3 tablespoons of the lemon juice.

2. In a large frying pan, heat the remaining 2 tablespoons oil over moderate heat. Add the onion and cook, stirring occasionally, until starting to brown, about 5 minutes. Add the cauliflower, garlic, and ¼ teaspoon of the salt and cook, stirring occasionally, until the cauliflower is golden, about 10 minutes. Add the saffron, if using, 1¼ teaspoons of the salt, ½ teaspoon of the pepper, the tomatoes, broth, and currants. Simmer until the cauliflower is tender, about 5 minutes. Stir in the couscous and parsley. Bring to a simmer. Cover, remove from the heat, and let sit for 5 minutes. Stir in the pine nuts and the remaining 1 tablespoon lemon juice.

3. Put the lamb on skewers. Sprinkle the kabobs with the remaining ½ teaspoon salt and ¼ teaspoon pepper. Grill or broil the kabobs, turning and basting with the marinade, until the lamb is cooked to your taste, 6 to 8 minutes for medium rare. Serve the skewers on the couscous.

FLORENTINE BEEFSTEAK

One of the simplest, yet most succulent dishes of Florence is the renowned *bistecca alla fiorentina*. Thick T-bone steaks of the highest quality and a very hot grill are the keys to success. Italians cook the steak rare and often douse it with a healthy squeeze of lemon. The combination of rich, red meat and tart juice is nothing short of exceptional. Do try it.

WINE RECOMMENDATION
There's nothing like a great steak to showcase a special, and if possible older, Barolo or Barbaresco. Made from the nebbiolo grape, these wines develop fabulously complex dried cherry, eucalyptus, floral, and truffle flavors along with a silky texture. Both have power to spare, but Barbaresco is more elegant.

SERVES 4

2 T-bone steaks, 1½ inches thick (about 4 pounds in all)

1 tablespoon olive oil

2 teaspoons salt

½ teaspoon fresh-ground black pepper

Lemon wedges, for serving

1. Light the grill. Rub the steaks with the oil and sprinkle with the salt and pepper.

2. Grill the steaks over high heat for 6 minutes. Turn and cook until done to your taste, about 6 minutes longer for rare. Serve with lemon wedges.

STEAK CHOICE

If you like, use **porterhouse** steaks instead of T-bones. Both of these bone-in steaks come from the short loin section of the animal. The bone separates the steak into strip loin and tenderloin sections. The strip loin has more flavor and the tenderloin is tenderer. Porterhouse steaks have more tenderloin and T-bones have a larger strip loin section. Choose according to your preference.

CHAPTER SEVEN

From
the Oven

ROASTED SWORDFISH AND POTATOES WITH CAPER MAYONNAISE

Ready-made mayonnaise is a bit sweet but tastes fine when balanced by acidic ingredients such as the vinegar and capers here. It's good with both the fish and potatoes.

WINE RECOMMENDATION

Though not a typical Italian wine, pinot noir is superb with swordfish. There are some tasty pinot noirs from the Alto Adige and Friuli, which you'll find under the Italian name pinot nero.

SERVES 4

1½ pounds boiling potatoes (about 4), cut into ½-inch pieces

½ cup olive oil

5 cloves garlic, chopped

½ teaspoon salt

½ teaspoon fresh-ground black pepper

4 swordfish steaks, about 1 inch thick (about 2 pounds in all)

1 teaspoon chopped fresh rosemary, or ½ teaspoon dried rosemary, crumbled

1 cup mayonnaise

2 tablespoons chopped fresh parsley

2 tablespoons drained chopped capers

1 teaspoon wine vinegar

1. Heat the oven to 400°. In a large roasting pan, toss the potatoes with ¼ cup of the oil, half the garlic, and ¼ teaspoon each salt and pepper. Put in the oven for 15 minutes; stir once.

2. Meanwhile, coat the swordfish with the remaining ¼ cup oil, garlic, ¼ teaspoon each salt and pepper, and the rosemary. Put the fish on a baking sheet and put it in the oven along with the potatoes. Cook, stirring the potatoes once, until the fish and potatoes are both done, 10 to 12 minutes for 1-inch-thick steaks.

3. In a small bowl, combine the mayonnaise with the parsley, capers, and vinegar. Serve the roasted swordfish and potatoes with the caper mayonnaise.

VARIATIONS

Try **tuna, salmon,** or **codfish** steaks instead of the swordfish. Fillets will also be good in this recipe, but you'll need to cut down on the cooking time. If you do, be sure the potatoes still cook for twenty-five minutes. Just put the fish in later.

Roast Chicken with Lemon, Oregano, and Vermouth

Simple roasted chicken parts are perfect for a weeknight meal. You'll have just enough concentrated jus to drizzle a little over each oregano-scented piece.

WINE RECOMMENDATION
This rustic, herbal roast chicken is best served with a full-bodied and strongly flavored white wine. Look to the south, where the earthy, richly nutty Greco di Tufo is found. Although virtually unknown, it's one of Italy's great whites.

SERVES 4

1   chicken (3 to 3½ pounds), cut into 8 pieces

4   teaspoons olive oil

1½ teaspoons dried oregano

2   tablespoons dry vermouth or white wine

1   teaspoon lemon juice

¼   teaspoon salt

⅛   teaspoon fresh-ground black pepper

2   tablespoons water

1. Heat the oven to 375°. Coat the chicken with 3 teaspoons of the oil. Put the pieces, skin-side up, in a large roasting pan. Sprinkle the chicken with the oregano, 1 tablespoon of the vermouth, the lemon juice, salt, and pepper. Drizzle the remaining teaspoon oil over the top.

2. Cook the chicken until the breasts are just done, about 25 minutes. Remove the breasts and wings and continue to cook the drumsticks and thighs until done, about 5 minutes longer.

3. Heat the broiler. Remove the roasting pan from the oven; return the breasts and wings to the pan. Broil the chicken until golden brown, about 2 minutes. Remove the chicken from the pan.

4. Pour off the fat from the roasting pan. Set the pan over moderate heat and add the remaining 1 tablespoon vermouth and the water. Bring to a boil, scraping the bottom of the pan to dislodge any brown bits. Boil until reduced to approximately 2 tablespoons. Add any accumulated juices from the chicken. Spoon the sauce over the chicken.

Variation

If you prefer **all white or dark meat**, use four bone-in breasts, eight drumsticks, or eight thighs instead of assorted pieces. Cook the breasts for twenty-five minutes or the legs for thirty minutes.

ROAST CHICKEN WITH BUTTERNUT SQUASH

Chicken quarters roasted with golden squash and sage are nice for a chilly autumn evening. To help the squash to brown evenly, be sure to spoon off the fat from the roasting pan after removing the breasts. This is a case where less is more: A thin layer of fat will brown the vegetable better than a quarter-inch of it.

WINE RECOMMENDATION
This winter-weight dish calls for a simple but robust red, and the sturdy Montepulciano d'Abruzzo, with its roasted-berry flavor, is just right. Best of all, it's among the least expensive of all Italian reds.

SERVES 4

1   chicken (3 to 3½ pounds), quartered

3   tablespoons olive oil

¾   teaspoon salt

¼   teaspoon fresh-ground black pepper

1   small butternut squash (about 2¼ pounds), peeled and cut into 1-inch cubes

1   teaspoon dried sage

3   tablespoons water

1. Heat the oven to 450°. Coat the chicken quarters with 1 tablespoon of the oil, ½ teaspoon of the salt, and ⅛ teaspoon of the pepper. Arrange the chicken quarters, skin-side up, in a large roasting pan. Toss the cubes of butternut squash with the remaining 2 tablespoons of oil, ¼ teaspoon of salt, and ⅛ teaspoon of pepper, and the sage. Add the cubes of squash to the roasting pan.

2. Cook, stirring the squash occasionally, until the chicken breasts are just done, about 20 minutes. Remove the pan from the oven and remove the breasts from the pan. Tilt the roasting pan and spoon off most of the fat from the pan. Return the pan to the oven. Continue cooking until the chicken legs and the squash are done, about 10 minutes longer. Remove the chicken and squash from the pan.

3. Pour off the fat from the roasting pan. Set the pan over moderate heat and add the water. Bring to a boil, scraping the bottom of the pan to dislodge any brown bits. Boil until reduced to approximately 2 tablespoons. Add any accumulated juices from the chicken. Spoon the sauce over the chicken.

VARIATIONS

■ Instead of the butternut, use your favorite winter squash, such as **acorn** or **Hubbard**— or, to be really Italian, try **pumpkin**.
■ Replace the chicken quarters with halved **Cornish hens**.

BAKED PORK CHOPS WITH SWISS CHARD

There's no need to brown the pork chops first; just pop them in the oven. As the chops bake, their juices will seep into the Swiss chard, flavoring the entire dish.

WINE RECOMMENDATION
Wines based on the sangiovese grape work particularly well with pork chops. Try a Vino Nobile di Montepulciano, similar to Chianti but richer, earthier, and more powerful.

SERVES 4

1 pound Swiss chard, stems removed, leaves washed and cut crosswise into 1-inch pieces

3 tablespoons olive oil

½ teaspoon salt

Fresh-ground black pepper

4 pork chops, about 1 inch thick (about 2 pounds in all)

1½ tablespoons grated Parmesan

2 ounces grated fontina (about ½ cup)

1. Heat the oven to 450°. Oil a 7½-by-11½-inch baking dish. In a medium bowl, toss the Swiss chard with 1 tablespoon of the oil, ¼ teaspoon of the salt, and ¼ teaspoon pepper. Put the chard in the baking dish.

2. Rub the pork chops with 1 tablespoon of the oil, the remaining ¼ teaspoon salt, and ⅛ teaspoon pepper. Put the pork chops on top of the Swiss chard. Drizzle the remaining tablespoon oil over the chard, around the pork chops.

Sprinkle the Parmesan and fontina over the chard, around the chops. Bake until the chops are just done, about 18 minutes. Let stand 5 minutes before serving.

SWISS CHARD

You can use either green or red Swiss chard for this dish. You'll want to rinse the leaves thoroughly before cooking, but don't dry them. The moisture will help keep the chard from drying out during cooking.

ROASTED GREEN-BEAN AND POTATO SALAD WITH SOPPRESSATA AND MOZZARELLA

Though it may remind you of an antipasti platter, this combination of cured meat, cheese, and roasted vegetables is substantial enough to be a main-dish salad. For a perfect final touch, have the cheese at room temperature, so that it will melt ever so slightly when tossed with the hot potatoes and beans.

WINE RECOMMENDATION
Franciacorta, made in Lombardy from an eclectic hodgepodge of grapes, is an offbeat choice but a good one. A lively, exuberantly fruity red wine, it partners salty foods well.

SERVES 4

    2   pounds small new potatoes
    1   pound green beans
 7½   tablespoons olive oil
    ¾   teaspoon salt
    2   teaspoons chopped fresh thyme, or
         ½ teaspoon dried thyme
    ¼   pound sliced *soppressata* or hard salami, cut
         into quarters
    ½   pound salted fresh mozzarella, cut into
         ½-inch cubes, at room temperature
    ½   cup chopped flat-leaf parsley
    ¼   teaspoon fresh-ground black pepper
    2   teaspoons lemon juice

1. Heat the oven to 450°. On a baking sheet, toss the potatoes with the green beans, 3½ tablespoons of the oil, ½ teaspoon of the salt, and the dried thyme, if using. Roast in the center of the oven for 20 minutes. Turn the potatoes and beans with a spatula and then sprinkle with the fresh thyme, if using. Roast until the vegetables are golden and tender, about 10 minutes longer. Transfer the vegetables to a large bowl.

2. Add the remaining 4 tablespoons oil and ¼ teaspoon salt, the *soppressata*, mozzarella, parsley, and pepper to the bowl and toss. Add the lemon juice and toss again. Let stand for 5 minutes to absorb the dressing before serving.

VARIATIONS

■ Line the plates with thin slices of **prosciutto** and top with the salad.
■ Add a roasted, peeled, seeded, and sliced **red bell pepper**.
■ Add a quarter cup of halved and pitted **black olives**.

PORTOBELLO-MUSHROOM AND RED-PEPPER PIZZA

Depending on the size of the appetites around your house, this substantial pizza with its meaty portobello mushrooms serves two very hungry people or four if it's accompanied by a big salad. If you don't have fresh basil, stir some pesto into the peppers and mushrooms before putting them on the pizza.

WINE RECOMMENDATION
Most dolcetto comes from two major centers in Piedmont: Asti, which produces lighter and sharper wines, and Alba, whose wines are rounder and fuller. Try the Alba version with this pizza.

MAKES ONE 14-INCH PIZZA

- 6 tablespoons olive oil
- 2 red bell peppers, cut into thin slices
- 1½ pounds portobello mushrooms, stems removed, caps cut into ¼-inch slices
- 1 teaspoon salt
- 1 pound store-bought or homemade pizza dough
- 3 cloves garlic, minced
- ¼ teaspoon fresh-ground black pepper
- ¾ cup lightly packed basil leaves, chopped
- ½ pound fresh salted mozzarella, cut into ¼-inch cubes
- ½ cup grated Parmesan

1. Heat the oven to 450°. In a large frying pan, heat 3 tablespoons of the oil over moderately high heat. Put the peppers in the pan and cook, stirring occasionally, for 10 minutes. Add the mushrooms and the salt and cook, stirring occasionally, until the mushrooms are golden, about 10 minutes more.

2. Meanwhile, oil a 14-inch pizza pan or large baking sheet. Press the pizza dough onto the pan in an approximately 14-inch round or 9-by-13-inch rectangle.

3. Spread the peppers and mushrooms on the pizza crust. Bake for 12 minutes. Sprinkle on the garlic, black pepper, and basil. Top with the mozzarella and then with the Parmesan. Drizzle with the remaining 3 tablespoons oil. Bake until the cheese is bubbling and beginning to brown, about 10 to 15 minutes longer.

EGGPLANT, PESTO, AND GOAT-CHEESE PIZZA

Tangy goat cheese, sharp Parmesan, tender sautéed eggplant, and bold pesto cover a mouth-watering pizza. As with the preceding recipe, this one makes a hearty fourteen-inch pizza; you be the judge whether it serves two or four.

WINE RECOMMENDATION
Sauvignon blanc is a remarkably versatile wine, and it's particularly delicious with goat cheese and basil. Once again, northeastern Italy is the place to look for these fresh, bracing wines.

MAKES ONE 14-INCH PIZZA

7½ tablespoons olive oil, or more as needed

1 1½- to 2-pound eggplant, cut into ¼-inch slices

¾ teaspoon salt

1 pound store-bought or homemade pizza dough

3 cloves garlic, minced

½ teaspoon fresh-ground black pepper

6 ounces mild goat cheese, such as Montrachet, cut into ¼-inch slices

½ cup grated Parmesan

½ cup store-bought or homemade pesto

1. Heat the oven to 450°. In a large non-stick frying pan, heat 2½ tablespoons of the oil over moderately high heat. Season the eggplant with the salt. Fry one-third of the eggplant, turning, until golden, about 10 minutes. Remove. Repeat in two more batches with the remaining oil, using more if needed, and eggplant.

2. Meanwhile, oil a 14-inch pizza pan or large baking sheet. Press the pizza dough onto the pan in an approximately 14-inch round or 9-by-13-inch rectangle.

3. Arrange the eggplant slices on the pizza crust. Sprinkle the garlic and pepper over the top. Bake for 12 minutes. Put the slices of goat cheese on the pizza, sprinkle with the Parmesan, and then dot with the pesto. Bake until the cheese begins to turn golden, about 15 minutes.

PIZZA DOUGH

Most supermarkets carry pizza dough; look for it in the refrigerator section. Another possibility is to ask for it at your favorite pizza restaurant. Many places are willing to sell it by the pound.

POTATO PIE WITH TOMATO AND FONTINA

It looks, smells, and tastes like pizza, with one delicious difference: The crust is made of mashed potatoes. You'll have to use a fork to eat this pie, since the slices aren't sturdy enough to hold in your hand.

WINE RECOMMENDATION
Barbera and dolcetto are the everyday workhorse wines of Piedmont. The more acidic and fruitier barbera is the better choice for dishes with a lot of tomatoes.

SERVES 4

2½   pounds baking potatoes (about 5), peeled and halved

1   28-ounce can tomatoes, drained and chopped fine (about 1 cup)

1¼   teaspoons salt

4   tablespoons olive oil

Fresh-ground black pepper

¾   pound grated fontina (about 3 cups)

3   cloves garlic, minced

5   anchovy fillets, minced

2   teaspoons dried oregano

⅓   cup grated Parmesan

1. Heat the oven to 450°. Put the potatoes in a medium saucepan of salted water. Bring to a boil, reduce the heat, and simmer until tender, about 20 minutes. Meanwhile, put the tomatoes in a strainer set over a medium bowl. Toss with ¾ teaspoon of the salt and let drain for 20 minutes.

2. Drain the potatoes and push them through a food mill, ricer, or strainer back into the saucepan. Cook over moderately low heat, stirring, until the potato starts to stick to the pan, about 5 minutes. Stir in 2 tablespoons of the oil, the remaining ½ teaspoon salt, and a pinch of pepper. Remove from the heat.

3. Oil a large baking sheet. Spread the potato mixture onto the baking sheet, forming two 6-by-11-inch rectangles. Top the potato with the fontina, leaving a ¼-inch border. Sprinkle the garlic and anchovies over the cheese. Top with the drained tomatoes followed by the oregano and Parmesan. Drizzle with the remaining 2 tablespoons oil. Bake the potato pies in the lower third of the oven until the cheese is bubbling and the edges are golden brown, about 25 minutes.

CHAPTER EIGHT

Simple Italian Desserts

PINEAPPLE CARPACCIO WITH LEMON SORBET AND CANDIED ZEST

Here's a refreshing dessert that looks and tastes spectacular. If you can find one, try a pineapple labeled *gold*; relatively new to the market, this hybrid is always lusciously sweet.

SERVES 4

  2 oranges

2¼ cups water

  ¾ cup sugar

  1 pineapple, chilled, peeled, and halved lengthwise

  1 pint lemon sorbet

  4 sprigs mint, for garnish (optional)

1. Using a vegetable peeler, cut the zest from one of the oranges in wide strips and then into matchstick strips. Put the zest in a medium saucepan with the water and sugar. Simmer until the zest is translucent and tender and the liquid is reduced to approximately ⅔ cup, about 25 minutes. Strain out the zest, reserving both the syrup and the zest. Squeeze ¾ cup juice from the oranges, strain into the syrup, and chill in the refrigerator.

2. Core each half of the pineapple by making a diagonal cut on one side of the core with a long serrated knife. Make a diagonal cut on the other side of the core, forming a V. Remove the core. Turn the halves over and cut the pineapple crosswise into ⅛-inch slices. Arrange the slices on four plates in concentric circles.

3. Pour the orange syrup over the pineapple slices. Put a scoop of sorbet on top of the pineapple and the candied zest over the sorbet. Garnish with the mint.

ESPRESSO GRANITA WITH WHIPPED CREAM

Top the granita with a hefty portion of whipped cream; you'll need the mild sweetness of the cream to balance the strong espresso. If you're cutting down on caffeine, you can use decaffeinated espresso beans instead of regular.

MAKES 1 PINT GRANITA

2 cups ground espresso beans

3 cups water

¼ cup plus 4 teaspoons sugar, or more to taste

⅔ cup heavy cream

1. Using an espresso machine, make coffee with the ground espresso and the water. You should have 1¾ cups strong espresso. Alternatively, make 1¾ cups espresso using a French press or drip coffee maker. Add the ¼ cup sugar and stir until dissolved. Taste the espresso and add more sugar if necessary. Chill in the refrigerator, or, to hasten the process, pour the espresso into a stainless-steel bowl, set it in a larger bowl filled with ice, and stir the coffee until cold.

2. Pour the chilled coffee into two 9-by-9-inch stainless-steel pans. Freeze for 15 minutes. Stir well and return the pans to the freezer. Continue freezing, stirring every 10 minutes, until the granita is completely frozen, about 40 minutes in all.

3. In a medium bowl, using a hand-held electric mixer, beat the cream with the remaining 4 teaspoons of sugar until the cream holds soft peaks when the beaters are lifted. Scoop the granita into chilled serving bowls and top with the whipped cream.

GRANITA TIPS

■ For extra speed, buy the espresso ready-made from a coffee shop.

■ You can put the warm espresso directly into the freezer, but it will take much longer to freeze.

■ Granita will freeze faster in a metal pan, but you can use Pyrex; just allow more time. Or freeze the liquid in metal bowls.

■ Stir the granita with a fork to get a nice fine grain.

■ Granita melts quickly, so serve it in bowls or glasses that have been chilled in the freezer.

HONEY-BAKED FIGS WITH ICE CREAM

Use purplish-black Mission figs, green-skinned Calimyrnas, or both for this great-tasting dessert. Give the figs a gentle squeeze to check for ripeness; they should be quite soft.

SERVES 4

12 fresh figs

1½ teaspoons olive oil

4 teaspoons honey

2 tablespoons cold butter, cut into 12 pieces

2 tablespoons water

1 pint vanilla ice cream

VARIATIONS

Sprinkle one-half cup chopped **walnuts** or **pistachios** over the figs after the first seven minutes of cooking.

1. Heat the oven to 425°. Cut the stems off the figs. Rub the oil over the figs and put them in a baking pan, stem-side up. Cut a cross in the top of each fig, cutting almost to the bottom.

2. Drizzle the honey over the figs. Top each one with a piece of the butter. Bake the figs until they open up like flowers, 8 to 10 minutes. Remove the pan from the oven.

3. Put the figs on plates, add the water to the pan, return the pan to the oven for 1 minute, and then stir to make a sauce. Drizzle the sauce over the warm figs and serve with a scoop of vanilla ice cream on the side.

RICOTTA ICE CREAM WITH HONEY AND ALMONDS

For an unusual but exceptionally easy dessert, soften a pint of vanilla ice cream, mix it with ricotta and honey, and then refreeze it. You'll want to use a premium brand of ice cream, since the quality of each ingredient is very apparent in this simple dessert.

MAKES 1½ PINTS

¾ cup sliced almonds
1 pint vanilla ice cream
1½ cups ricotta cheese
½ cup honey

1. In a small frying pan, toast the almonds over moderately low heat, stirring frequently, until golden brown, about 5 minutes. Or toast them in a 350° oven for 5 to 10 minutes. Let cool completely.

2. Put a large metal bowl in the freezer. Let the ice cream stand at room temperature until just beginning to soften but still frozen. In a food processor, puree the ricotta and honey until smooth.

3. Remove the bowl from the freezer and put the ice cream in it. Stir until smooth. Stir in the ricotta mixture. Transfer the ice-cream mixture to a shallow stainless-steel pan and then return it to the freezer, covered, until firm enough to scoop, about 60 minutes. Serve the ice cream topped with the toasted almonds.

ZABAGLIONE WITH STRAWBERRIES

Here we serve the zabaglione hot when it's just made, but if you want to prepare the dish ahead of time, mix the zabaglione with whipped cream and refrigerate it as described in the first variation below.

SERVES 4

8 large egg yolks, at room temperature

¾ cup dry marsala

½ cup sugar

1 pint strawberries, sliced

1. Put the egg yolks, the marsala, and then the sugar into a large stainless-steel bowl. Set the bowl over a large saucepan filled with 1 inch of barely simmering water. Using a hand-held electric mixer on low speed or a whisk, beat the egg-yolk mixture until it is hot and the mixture forms a ribbon when the beaters are lifted, 5 to 8 minutes. Don't cook the zabaglione for too long, or it will curdle.

2. Put the strawberries in stemmed glasses or in bowls. Top with the hot zabaglione and either serve the dessert immediately or refrigerate it for up to an hour.

VARIATIONS

■ For a zabaglione that will last up to six hours in the refrigerator, add **whipped cream**. Beat half a cup of heavy cream just until it holds firm peaks. When the zabaglione is done, remove the bowl from the heat and continue beating until it's cool. Fold the cooled zabaglione into the whipped cream. Put the strawberries in bowls, top with the zabaglione, and refrigerate.

■ Substitute **blueberries**, **raspberries**, or sliced **peaches** for the strawberries.

TEST-KITCHEN TIP

What you need to make zabaglione is, in effect, a double boiler that's wide enough to accommodate an electric mixer. This is easy to rig up with a heatproof bowl set over a saucepan.

CHERRIES POACHED IN RED WINE WITH MASCARPONE CREAM

Thick mascarpone cheese mixed with honey makes a luscious topping for poached cherries. You can serve the dessert either warm or cold. We love it both ways.

SERVES 4

2¼ cups red wine

1 cup sugar

1 1-by-3-inch strip orange zest

2 pounds sweet cherries, halved and pitted

1 cup mascarpone cheese

2½ tablespoons honey

1. In a medium stainless-steel saucepan, combine the wine, sugar, and orange zest. Bring to a simmer over moderately high heat. Add the cherries and bring back to a simmer. Reduce the heat and simmer, partially covered, until the cherries are just tender, about 5 minutes. Pour into a glass or stainless-steel bowl so the cherries don't overcook.

2. In a small bowl, combine the mascarpone with the honey. Remove the strip of orange zest from the cherries. Serve the warm cherries and syrup in bowls or stemmed glasses, topped with a large dollop of the mascarpone cream.

VARIATIONS

- The warm cherries and poaching liquid are great alone—without the mascarpone cream—or with **whipped cream**.
- Serve the mascarpone cream with cut up **fresh fruit** or **mixed berries** instead of with the poached cherries.

BAKED PEACHES WITH ALMOND PASTE

Stuff ripe, juicy peach halves with pureed almond paste and then bake them until tender and golden. Puree the almond mixture ahead of time if you like, but wait until the last minute to cut and stuff the peaches, or they'll turn brown.

SERVES 4

4 peaches, halved and pitted

6 ounces almond paste (about ½ cup)

3 tablespoons hot water

1 teaspoon lemon juice

1½ teaspoons cold butter, cut into 8 pieces

1. Heat the oven to 400°. Put a rack on a baking sheet and then put the peaches on the rack, skin-side down.

2. In a food processor, puree the almond paste, water, and lemon juice. Spoon the almond mixture into the centers of the peaches. Top each mound of almond paste with a piece of the butter.

3. Bake in the lower third of the oven until the peaches are tender and the almond paste is golden brown, about 25 minutes. Serve warm.

PEELING THE PEACHES

Peel the peaches or not, as you like. The blush on the skin is pretty, but during taste tests most of us pulled off the peel and pushed it to the side of the plate.

ALMOND PASTE

Almond paste is simply a combination of ground almonds and sugar. It's available in supermarkets, usually in the baking aisle, and comes in both cans and tubes.

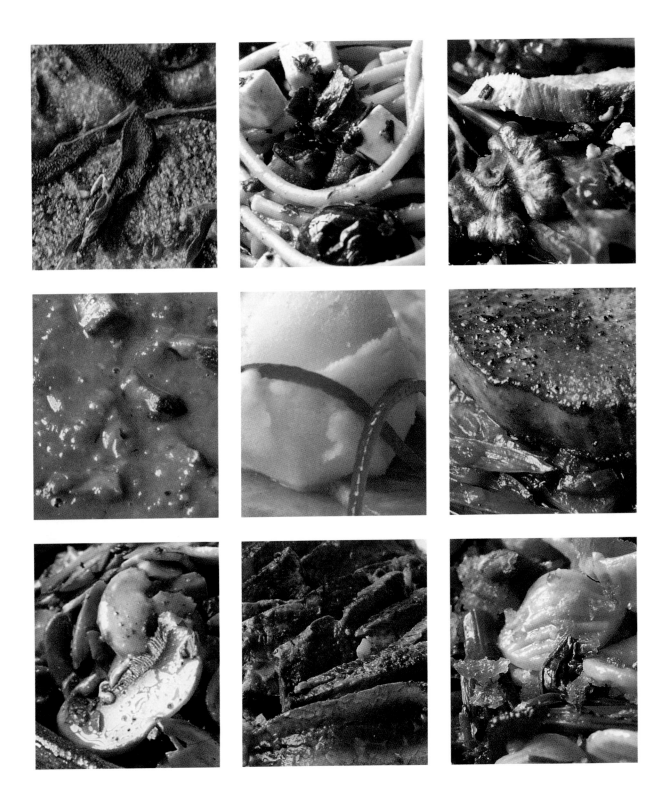

ESSENTIAL ITALIAN INGREDIENTS

Anchovies

Give anchovies a chance; they give a dish tremendous depth of flavor. Use salt-packed, jarred, or canned anchovies, or even anchovy paste—whichever form you prefer. Half a teaspoon of anchovy paste equals two flat anchovy fillets.

Bread Crumbs

Bread crumbs, either dry or fresh, are used as a coating for fried meat and fish and as a topping for pasta and crusty vegetable gratins. Making fresh bread crumbs is simple: Put pieces of bread in the food processor and give it a whir.

Broth

Italians generally make broth from a combination of meat and chicken. However, we developed all of the recipes in this book using canned low-sodium chicken broth. You can substitute regular for low-sodium broth, if you prefer; just cut back on the salt in the recipe. Of course, if you keep homemade chicken stock or meat broth in the freezer, by all means use it.

Capers

These tart Mediterranean flower buds add piquancy to a dish. Since they come bottled in a vinegary brine, you'll want to drain them before use. We use small nonpareil capers in these recipes; if you use larger ones, just chop them first.

Cornmeal

Cornmeal is ground from dried kernels of yellow or white corn. Its texture ranges from powdery to quite coarse; you'll want to use a medium- or coarse-textured cornmeal for making polenta. We don't recommend instant polenta, which often has seasonings and dried vegetables added to it.

Garlic

Although garlic is commonly associated with Italian cooking, use just enough of it to flavor a dish, not enough to kill a vampire. Keep in mind that the size of garlic cloves varies tremendously; when we call for one minced or chopped clove, we expect you to get about three quarters of a teaspoon. When cooking with garlic, be careful to never let it burn or it will taste bitter.

RECIPES PICTURED OPPOSITE: (top) pages 105, 57, 135; (center) pages 41, 167, 113; (bottom) pages 19, 145, 73

Herbs

Italian cooking makes frequent use of basil, bay leaves, marjoram, oregano, flat-leaf parsley, rosemary, sage, and thyme. Use only fresh basil, parsley, and marjoram; they don't dry well. In fact, basil is best not only fresh but raw, added to warm dishes only at the last minute. Besides these three, the other herbs retain their character when dried, so you can use them confidently in either form.

Lemon Juice

Fresh-squeezed lemon juice adds bright acidity to dressings, marinades, grilled meats and fish, and cooked or raw vegetables. Not only is lemon juice an ingredient in many recipes, but lemon wedges are frequently served alongside the dish so the diner can add a final burst of flavor and aroma just before eating.

Olive Oil

As a cornerstone of the Italian kitchen, olive oil appears in virtually every part of the meal. Choose an extra-virgin oil, which comes from the first cold pressing of the olives, to use in both salads and in cooking. Olive oil doesn't age well; store it in a cool, dry place and try to use it within a year. When the oil loses its bright, fresh scent and starts to smell like cardboard, it's rancid.

Olives

If your store doesn't sell olives from big, open barrels, opt for the kind in jars. The canned version gives you only the slightest hint of what a good olive might taste like.

Pasta, Dry

With hundreds of shapes to choose from, dry pasta is a lifesaver when you want to make dinner quickly. Flour-and-water pasta, such as spaghetti and macaroni, is virtually always bought dried, even in Italy. Egg pasta (all the flat types, like fettuccine and pappardelle) can be glorious fresh, but unless you're going to make your own—definitely not a quick task—dried is a better bet than most store-bought fresh, which tends to be mushy, flavorless, or both, as well as more expensive.

Pepper

There's nothing like fresh-ground black pepper. If you've been using preground, buy a pepper mill, fill it, and give it a grind. You'll never look back.

Pine Nuts

Pine nuts come from pine cones. The pignoli from Italy, Spain, and Portugal are more desirable than the nuts from China (which have a stronger pine flavor), but they're also considerably more expensive. The Chinese ones are fine for most cooking.

Porcini Mushrooms, Dried

Since fresh porcini mushrooms are seasonal and quite expensive, the dried version is a handy alternative. Dried porcini are available in small packages weighing about an ounce, and they keep indefinitely. Their flavor is concentrated and intense. Put the mushrooms in warm water to reconstitute them before using. After a soak, remove the mushrooms from the liquid, rinse, and dry them before continuing with the recipe. Save the soaking liquid to enhance risottos, soups, and sauces.

Prosciutto

The remarkable balance of sweetness and saltiness gives prosciutto great appeal. Prosciutto is pork that has been salt cured and air-dried; it is never smoked. Due to its full, satisfying flavor, a little goes a long way in cooking.

Rice, Arborio

Arborio rice appears in Italian soups and boiled rice dishes, but plays its major role in risotto. The short, stubby grains contain loads of starch, which is released into the broth during cooking. Risotto makes its own sauce of thickened, creamy broth.

Tomatoes

If you plan to use fresh tomatoes, be sure they are vine ripened to a full red. If you can't find good ones, use high-quality canned, peeled plum tomatoes. Many domestic brands, as well as those imported from the San Marzano region in Italy, are excellent and are available in supermarkets.

Tuna, Canned

Tuna packed in olive oil is more moist and flavorful than water-packed, perfect for salads, sauces, and antipasti. You can drain off the oil from the tuna or add it to what you're cooking; the tuna-impregnated olive oil will heighten the taste of the dish.

Vinegar

In general, use either red- or white-wine vinegar for cooking and for salads. Balsamic vinegar, which can range from heavenly to horrible, is added sparingly to dishes toward the end of cooking, or combined with other vinegars for green salads. Look for balsamic vinegar from Modena, aged if possible.

Wine

Wine is nearly as essential to Italian cooking as it is to French. Often a bit of a bottle is used for braising meat or making a simple pan sauce, and then the remainder is served with the meal. Or the end of yesterday's bottle can be put to good use in today's cooking. Dry vermouth can be used as an alternative to dry white wine.

INDEX

Page numbers in **boldface** indicate photographs   🍇 indicates wine recommendations